How to Start a Blog

Learn the Best Techniques to Start Blogging Now. Turn Your Fans into Your Passive Income.

By Jim Norton

of this publication is strictly prohibited and any storage of this document is not allowed unless with written permission from the publisher. All rights reserved.

The information provided herein is stated to be truthful and consistent, in that any liability, in terms of inattention or otherwise, by any usage or abuse of any policies, processes, or directions contained within is the solitary and utter responsibility of the recipient reader. Under no circumstances will any legal responsibility or blame be held against the publisher for any reparation, damages, or monetary loss due to the information herein, either directly or indirectly.

Respective authors own all copyrights not held by the publisher.

The information herein is offered for informational purposes solely and is universal as so. The presentation of the information is without contract or any type of guarantee assurance.

The trademarks that are used are without any consent, and the publication of the trademark is without permission or backing by the trademark owner. All trademarks and brands within this book are for clarifying purposes only and are the owned by the owners themselves, not affiliated with this document.

Table of Contents

What Is A Blog? 7

How to Start a Blog.....................13

Profiting with Blogs 25

Measuring a Blog's Success 41

Niche Blogging......................53

Setting Up Your Blog...................67

Blog Design Considerations 91

Blog Writing 95

Types of Blog Posts 119

Steps to Writing a Successful Series on Your Blog ..131

Blog Promotion and Marketing 153

Search Engine Optimization for Blogs...................167

Social Media and Your Blog...................183

Planning for Sustainable Growth...................195

Secrets of Successful Blogs 203

Author's Final Thoughts 215

Chapter One

What Is A Blog?

A Guide to Understanding the Idea of Blogging

Many people who have heard the term "blogging" do not understand what a "blog" is or how they create or read one can affect or improve their life. If you have no idea what these terms stand for or if you know the basics but want to know more, this guide offers a detailed breakdown of the topic.

You like blogging. You can call it a hobby, but the truth is that it's your passion. Your blog wakes you up in the morning, taking you out of bed with the magnetic allure of its power to share your thoughts with the world. At night, it keeps you up to date with a range of ideas you don't stop at. This should be important if your blog is about raising children or finances or deep-sea fish; The point is that you can write about what matters most to you.

And it turns out, he says pretty well. You have readers. People are really interested in what you have to say. You discovered a community you never knew existed: people who share your passion. That's an amazing thing. But do you know what would surprise you even more? If you can make money blogging.

The following sections also provide details on popular blog sites and how to use one or more blogs to raise funds for personal and professional purposes.

So Exactly *What Is a Blog*?

A blog is a newspaper, or an online newspaper located on a website. Blog content typically includes text, images, videos, animated GIFs, and even analysis of old newspapers or offline physical magazines and other paper documents. Because a blog can exist for personal use only, share information with an exclusive group, or involve the public, the blog owner can configure his blog for public or private access.

When a blog is publicly available, anyone can find it through links available on the blog owner's individual or professional website, their profiles on social networks, emails and newsletters, and online search engines for keywords. , Many blog owners have also created blogs on websites dedicated to creating, storing and sharing blogs, such as Blogger, LiveJournal, Tumblr and WordPress.

Blog content may appear as a publication on a download page or a publication on individual pages accessible through one or more pages configured as a list in the form of links to the titles of publications, snippets and associated tags. , All articles or links to articles are usually presented to readers in reverse order, with the most recent content appearing first.

History of the Blog

Blogs began as a natural extension of greater use of computers and the creation of the first forms of the Internet as a military, scientific and academic network of government. Before the world wide web, groups of people communicated on these networks. People have created content for themselves or others and stored it on computers connected to networks. Before blogging became popular, these communities often communicated and shared frequently updated content through community bulletin boards. The term "focus groups" is coined to describe many of these areas of discussion and exchange of information.

The first real blogs began to appear around 1994 or 1995 in the form of open access journals in which people shared news about life, such as personal reflections and facts about family events, university studies. , careers, travel and other subjects. The first authors of online newspapers include Claudio Pinhanez, Justin Hall and Carolyn Burke. The media and the public really began to notice the content and documented their training around 1996 and 1997.

Scholars are still deliberating the exact date and year of first use of the term "blog". Most believe that this happened in 1999 as a natural shortening of a particular description of this type of content, "web magazine" or "blog," in abbreviated form. There is a debate over pronunciation. Obviously, the term describes a newspaper or newspaper that is and is available on the World Wide Web. Over time, some people thought that "weblog" should be pronounced "we blog" to refer to the people running the blogging business.

Chapter Two

How to Start a Blog

The generation of "Internet users" has created a world of cyberspace where anyone can do anything at any time. If there is something made possible by the Internet, people are heard online. There are social networks to connect with friends, online videos to promote yourself and teaching, blogs for people who love to write.

Blogs have been redefined over the years, and bloggers around the world have also become a different internet class. Simply put, a blog basically consists of writing about everything online, comparable to writing a newspaper or magazine. What are the steps to start a blog? There are millions of online tips that could teach you how to start a blog, but there are easy ways to do it.

Find Your Blogger Identity.

Simply put, you need to find your niche. "What kind of blogger do you want to be?" Before creating a blog, it's an important question. There are different types of bloggers online and they talk about almost every topic known to man; Bloggers who talk about fashion, technology, sports, music, movies, food, travel or just about their daily lives. Different writers have found their niche by writing what they like and what interests them and their audience.

If there is something that keeps people from getting ahead with the beginning of a blog, then fear is whether it will be interesting enough for people to read. Don't think and analyze too much. Just write down what you like, and people are likely to love it too.

Choose a Blog Platform

After deciding what type of blog you want to build, choose your blog platform to host your blog site. There are many websites that offer free hosting such as Blogger, WordPress or Tumblr. These blog hosting sites allow you to blog for free and sometimes help you start a blog. These blog hosting sites even let you to store the photos you want to include in your posts.

Choose the right blog site to meet your needs, but if you have no idea, you can always read reviews online and see what people think of those sites.

The Name Game

In the blogging world, your name is your identity. Other bloggers will identify and associate it with this name. You should think of your name as a brand, in the long run, when your blog has more loyal readers and followers, it will be promoted to other bloggers by that name. Make sure the name is unique and really represents who you are or what it says in your blog. Take the mysterious, beautiful names or be the unannounced blogger by simply using your name.

Get Yourself Out There

Depending on whether you are writing on a particular topic or talking about personal matters, the main reason for your blog is to share and be listened to. Promote your blog to readers via social networks, post links to your new articles. The word will eventually come out of the new blog until it reaches the target audience. And, in the long run, your readership will grow, you can even benefit from it.

Blogs are open to anyone who wants to write, whether it's a professional writer or just writing to express themselves, take the step to begin their blog journey.

What Is the Difference Between Blogs and Websites?

The main difference between a blog and a web site is that the blog is a specific type of content that is displayed on the web pages of the web site. Confusion often happens because people and sales reps often use these two terms interchangeably. For example, one might say that he visited a corporate blog when, in fact, the blog was only part of the company's website. Confusion also happens because blog-only platforms create the impression that the blog of a person or company on one of those platforms is also their main website.

To resolve this, keep in mind: In most cases, non-blog sites are updated with new content less frequently than associated blog pages and dedicated blogs. Blogs generally receive updates weekly, daily, or even less than an hour. Non-blog sites, such as personal interests and biographical or commercial websites, usually only update the news and blog content at that interval and then add new pages or update the content as needed. Blogs also encourage discussion. There are comment sections designed to create online conversations about blog content and blog owners in the same way as comment sections that provide readership to media platforms and other publishers.

The Difference between Pages and Blog Posts

In other words, the blog content that opens in your program shows up on the site page. The term "page" portrays the archive and its area. It's basic to remember that the term "blog" is regularly used to portray a collection of websites that explicitly share blog content, particularly blog-situated websites. This use is like the manner in which people depict a collection of pages in a paper, magazine or paper altogether as a subject. As referenced before, blog content is regularly updated. Numerous websites have non-blog pages that contain content that once in a while changes, for example, a history page or a business page. A few websites have not been updated after some little, updated and new content changes throughout the years.

Popularity of Blogs and Blogging

Many people wonder why blogs and blogs are so well known. Blogs offer a social outlet. Many are, commonly, social creatures. They were searching for others online to interact and share information and viewpoints. Indeed, even numerous people who are face-to-face with withdrawn, disconnected designs like to convey online through interpersonal organizations utilizing their genuine characters or mysterious people. Since a blog is a social instrument, making or blogging first gives a superior elective strategy to interacting with others that didn't exist previously.

In addition, social and reserved people use blogs to make new friends and different types of connections and to more readily comprehend the lives of people who may not convey every day. For instance, blogs offer them the chance to interact with people from different societies and/or who live in other geographic locales, people who work in various expert fields, and people who have utilized types of sections - Time is as of now geologically restricted and uncommon. Today, blogs offer a request that people don't discover in the past simply through papers, magazines, TV appears, films, narratives, and exceptional disconnected festivals supported by networks and organizations. , expressions associations, neighborhood, state and governments and scholarly establishments.

What Sort of People Blog?

There are no confinements on the types of people who make blogs. Blog makers, likewise, called "bloggers", originate from varying backgrounds and from all pieces of the world. Up to one approaches online apparatus that assist them with making website content, they can make a blog and elevate it to pull in users. The most widely recognized bloggers incorporate people who essentially need to share individual information about themselves and/or their inclinations and leisure activities with the world.

A few people utilize this web content apparatus to bring issues to light of issues they believe are critical to improving others, for example, political news issues, philanthropies, security issues, pet consideration, and wellbeing conditions. Organizations by and large use blogs to improve the lives of their clients when all is said in done, show them how to utilize items/benefits securely and cause to notice their involvement with a specific industry or their items/administrations.

For What Reason Do People Try Blogging?

People blog for a wide variety of reasons, aside from those as of now referenced. Numerous people basically don't care for conventional paper composing disconnected and need an outlet for their considerations and sentiments past this format, face-to-face interactions, telephone calls, or online talk. Some prefer to have the option to share their increasingly personal musings and information with others on the opposite side of the world. Some of the time such an outlet is attractive in light of the fact that they have no friends or disconnected emotionally supportive network and use blogs to assist them with adapting to distressing life occasions, for example, intense and interminable medical issues. or then again grieving after the demise of friends and family.

Since numerous different forms of content on various websites don't require visit refreshes, numerous people, particularly entrepreneurs, utilize their blogs as a major aspect of their engine enhancement devices to keep up or improve the positioning of their outcomes. Web indexes likewise produce more traffic to your sites. Internet searcher calculations assess new and important content over past content, and when a site gets more traffic, the site proprietor is bound to build income.

What Makes Blogs Different?

If blogs are simply websites, what makes them so unique? As I would see it there are three fundamental territories that separate a blog from some other kind of site:

- Content — Blogs are generally updated more frequently than customary websites are; many are updated on different occasions a day, and this keeps guests returning all the more regularly. The content is additionally ordinarily masterminded backward sequential request with the latest "post" (article) at the highest point of the principle page and the more seasoned passages toward the base.

- Syndication — Not just can blog adherents read a blog in their internet browser simply like they can some other website, a blog more likely than not gives the content as a "feed." as such, the articles presented on the site are given in a machine-discernible format, enabling people with the proper programming to peruse the blog posts as they are distributed without really visiting the site.

- Conversation — The style of a blog is very not the same as different types of websites; there is to a greater extent a conversational and network feel. In contrast to an absolutely informational site, or a customary news site, blogs are composed with the bloggers imparting straightforwardly to their crowd, and answers are normal as remarks. In addition to the discussion occurring on each blog, discussion likewise occurs between blogs, with one blog post pulling in answers and reactions on others.

The Added Benefits of Blogging

Indeed, blogging has numerous advantages. Although numerous bloggers get delight just from the way toward composing, and obviously we can't disregard the bloggers who profit, blogging may assist you with accomplishing different objectives:

- Fame — An effective blog can possibly get you saw and assist you with building an increasingly unmistakable profile in your business market, hobby, or network

- Contacts — Blogs are phenomenal approaches to become more acquainted with people and system. Since blogs normally lead to discussion, a well-perused blog will place you in contact with a wide assortment of people.

- Traffic — Attracting profoundly focused on guests alone could be a major draw, particularly if you have items or administrations to sell. Website proprietors are continually searching for new wellsprings of traffic, and blogs are a demonstrated method to create more visits and expanded dedication.

- Sales — In addition to increasing more consideration, after some time through your articles you can create trust and manufacture validity, basic to making deals.

Chapter Three

Profiting with Blogs

We've just referenced two or multiple times that blogs can profit, yet so far, we have offered no clarification of how that is the situation. This area investigates how bloggers profit. While you read this, you might need to consider strategies that intrigue to you.

Prologue to Professional Blogging

In the course of recent years blogging has changed a lot and developed from numerous points of view. What was before an action constrained to few people has now detonated into a smaller than expected industry. As the quantity of bloggers has detonated, so has the quantity of apparatuses and administrations accessible for bloggers.

Online exercises that once included a decent arrangement of constancy and a great deal of specialized capability would now be able to be rapidly and effectively performed by anybody with a couple of snaps and some composing. Web distributing has landed for the general population. With these advancements and a developing mindfulness, a few people have prevailing with regards to benefitting from their blogs. To start with it was practically unfathomable for somebody to win cash from their blog; truth be told, for some, benefit was viewed as counter to blogging society. This before long changed. As the primary pioneers shared their pay accomplishments the concentration after profiting from blogging has expanded. Presently, although monetary profit probably won't be normal, it is surely considerably more acknowledged.

Over ongoing years, the term "proficient blogger" landed to depict any individual who approaches blogging not as just a leisure activity, yet as an expert cash winning movement.

The Amount Could You Earn?

It ought to be worried before we go any further that bloggers need to go into an assessment of this subject with reasonable desires. While a huge number of bloggers are trying different things with proficient blogging, most bloggers are not getting rich and are just enhancing their salary by blogging. Although a few bloggers like Darren and I do bring home the bacon from blogging, and there are bloggers who clear a path more than both of us do, a lot more bloggers utilize their blogging pay to sponsor contraption buys or to counterbalance some Internet costs. Much the same as in many different backgrounds, the individuals who succeed are the rare sorts of people who invest the push to find success with it as time goes on, though most others fall by the wayside before they truly get moving.

Ace Blogging Is Not a Get-Rich-Quick Tactic

It once in a while frustrates people when we guide them to look somewhere else If they need moment wealth. Sadly, for the eager, it sets aside effort to construct a gainful blog. You don't simply turn into an expert blogger medium-term anything else than you in a split second become an expert golf player. If solitary this was the situation! Despite the fact that blogging includes you settling on a choice that you will win cash from blogging; it is additionally something you need to progress in the direction of after some time. Truly, you could rake in some serious cash from blogging. Peruse the tales that are going around on blogs of people making good full-time wages from blogging and you will get a thought of the kind of procuring potential that exists. Take care likewise to find out about and research the difficult work and time venture required by bloggers who have made a monetarily reasonable blog. Recollect that for each well-pitched example of overcoming adversity you do find out about, there are a lot of others around who have attempted and bombed that you don't find out about. There are much more people who battle to make anything else than a couple of dollars from their blogs than who win those features making five-figures-a-month sums. Try not to misunderstand us; we aren't not saying this to hose the fervor and dreams of genius bloggers! The general purpose of this book is to assist you with accomplishing precisely those fantasies, yet we think it is the duty of those of us who wands, no shrouded stunts, and no mystery handshakes that can bring your prompt achievement, yet with time, vitality, and determination you can arrive.

Immediate and Indirect Earning Methods

We really expound on precisely how you can gain cash from a blog later in this book, however profiting from blogging is accomplished with two general classifications of strategies: immediate and circuitous adaptation. Most blogs and bloggers will in general utilize either of these techniques, yet there is nothing to prevent bloggers from exploring different avenues regarding components of both. Direct Monetization Direct techniques incorporate procedures that empower bloggers to win a salary straightforwardly from their blogs. Models incorporate the accompanying:

- Advertising

- Sponsorships

- Affiliate commissions

- Paid surveys (If you are gotten by Google selling joins you can lose your rankings.)

- Indirect Monetization

Indirect techniques incorporate those in which bloggers win an income in view of their blog. This could be taking your blog-inferred authority, validity, and mastery and utilizing it for any of the accompanying:

- Freelance agreements

- Books and digital books

- Speaking commitment

- Consultancy openings

- Service contracts

- Running courses, classes, and workshops

- Membership sites and paid networks

Detached and Active Income

A major intrigue for making money out of blogs, or in reality web distributing by and large, is that numerous people consider it to be an easy revenue or income that is earned in any event, when they are not effectively working. Despite the fact that there are viewpoints to blogging that can be viewed as permitting an easy revenue — for instance, publicizing can procure you money while you are snoozing, you can take vacation days, etc. — in established truth you do need to continue working at it to make a relentless or expanding income. Blogs that stay still, don't get thought about, or are clearly worked with computerized or ripped-off content eventually decay and vanish. At the point when a blog draws in no guests, the blogger won't procure income.

Is Pro Blogging Right for You?

Darren and I address bloggers consistently who have heard the accounts of blogs that make large money and who need to attempt to make an income from blogging. One of the suggestions that we offer, knowing very well indeed that it doesn't generally traverse, is that it merits requiring some investment out to ask yourself in the case of making money with a blog is directly for you. Despite the fact that this may appear to be a senseless or in any event, offending inquiry to a few, it is intended to assist you with analyzing your aims. Only one out of every odd blogger is fit to blogging for money. Numerous new bloggers find that from the outset the eagerness and thoughts come effectively, however after the primary flush of vitality has passed it gets harder and harder to compose each day, not to mention stay aware of the various exercises required to keep up a blog. At the point when your income relies upon keeping it up, you may discover a portion of the sentiments of fervor and happiness have gone to disdain and blogging has become a task.

Which Monetization Method Is Right for You?

It isn't constantly evident which style of adaptation you should pursue. Every adaptation strategy is fitting to an alternate style of blog and blogger. Think about the accompanying ways to deal with blogging and check whether they fit you. We have noted which class they fundamentally fall under.

Indirect

Here are some common reasons for blogging that fall in the aberrant adaptation class:

- You blog to help promote your business.

- You blog since you need to sell your products.

- You blog since you need to promote your composition.

- You blog since you need to make yourself known.

Direct

Here are some common reasons for blogging that fall in the immediate adaptation classification:

- You blog for recreational purposes, about your inclinations and leisure activities.

- You blog to make money in your extra time.

- You blog about products and compose audits.

Presently, there is nothing amiss with blogging for more than one explanation and a blend of methodologies is unquestionably conceivable, however bloggers considering adding income streams to their blogs should know about the likelihood that the ramifications of going toward that path may affect their different objectives. Let me share a few scenarios of genuine cases that Darren and I have gone over where putting promotions on a blog was anything but a smart thought. Despite the fact that they may appear to be explicit, I am certain they speak to the account of numerous bloggers and that you can envision a lot more scenarios.

Business Blogs Advertising for Competitors

Numerous businesspeople loathe the idea of leaving money on the table, so when they catch wind of blog advertising, they think they have figured out how to make money from squandered traffic. Truth be told, what will in general happen is that the ads that are served up by their blogs are for other contending organizations in their field. Despite the fact that they could obstruct a portion of the ads, regularly more ads come in to supplant them.

If you are advancing your own products or administrations, be incredibly cautious about showing flags or any offers other than your own. By and large the space you give over to advertising could be all the more productively used to sell your very own offering.

The Most Effective Method to Make Blog Advertising Work for You

- Here are the key tips for considering blog advertising:

- Put your user and content first.

- Don't allow ads to rule.

- Ensure just pertinent and proper ads are shown.

- Write audits just for products that you have utilized.

- Promote member offers just when you are certain they are great worth. (Uncover your associate relationship so as not to fall foul of the FTC guidelines.)

Blog Strategies

At the point when they consider earning money from blogging, numerous people consider just one model:

1. Set up a blog.

2. Make it well known.

3. Earn from advertising.

Multiple Blogs

Above all else there is no motivation behind why you ought to have just one blog. Darren and I each have a few blogs. Despite the fact that your earnings on an individual blog probably won't set the world land, if you have multiple blogs and earn two or three hundred dollars for each blog, it could make for a significant decent compensation.

Independent Blogging

In addition to owning my own blogs, I make a level of my income composing for others. It is agreeable, can be worthwhile, and is really incredible advertising for my very own blog and me. Clearly, I think it is a decent arrangement for the blogger, however shouldn't something be said about the individual procuring the blogger? People hire an independent blogger to blog for them for a few reasons:

Capacity

There is simply the composition and afterward the various things a blogger needs to do, for example, traffic building and advancement, structure changes, specialized stuff like introducing modules and programming, etc.

Time

If you are caught up with maintaining your business yet you realize you would profit by a blog, at that point you may hire another person to do the genuine composition. I know numerous bloggers who have developed smaller than normal systems of blogs along these lines without doing a significant part of the real blogging.

System

As you will see later in this book, achievement can be as reliant on others as all alone endeavors. Here and there people hire different bloggers who they know are well-associated with access people and networks generally distant for them. Information At times you may require a topic master to compose on specific subjects. Instead of learning everything yourself, you can redistribute those articles.

Credibility

Enlisting an effectively well-known blogger is additionally a bit of leeway since you can use their credibility and traffic to support your own. There's not at all like having an outstanding, enormous name blogger to drive people to your site.

Build and Flip

An idea natural in reality land market, building and flipping has moved over to the virtual world of property advancement. Basically, it is conceivable to grow a blog's esteem and afterward sell it. You could build without any preparation or locate an immature property, get it, give it a makeover, and afterward sell it for a benefit.

Chapter Four

Measuring a Blog's Success

If you are building a blog to earn money directly, or If you are planning to make deals from your blog, at that point money is your undeniable metric to determine how well you are getting along. Imagine a scenario in which direct income or prospective customers are not part of your arrangement. How might you measure the success of your blog at that point? Each blogger you address appears to have a unique point of view on what determines a successful blog. For some it could be about traffic, others organize the number of supporters, and a few bloggers consider remarks the best measure. Every metric method various thing to various people. The accompanying segments spread a couple of measures of success that various bloggers use to evaluate how their blogs are going. Some will be pretty much pertinent for various blogs and will rely on the objectives and goals of the blogger.

Traffic

The most common ways that bloggers use to evaluate a blog are the various measures of traffic. Various bloggers appear to have their very own inclinations with respect to various parts of traffic, in addition to each apparatus you use to measure traffic gives an alternate outcome because of the varying philosophies utilized. It is uncommon to discover two distinct instruments that agree on any one outcome, so when estimating traffic, it is ideal to adhere to your preferred help and use it to show progress instead of fixating on the real numbers.

Unique Visitors

The idea behind following unique visitors is to check the number of people who visit your blog. The issue in determining this precisely is there is no real way to realize who is visiting with any certainty except if you get every individual to sign in each time they read. To get a harsh idea of what number of unique people visit a blog, you can utilize methods, for example, checking every unique IP address (a number given to every gadget associated with the Internet) or recording "treats" (little content passages spared by your web browser for later recovery). All techniques have advocates and issues. For instance, your IP address today may be diverse tomorrow, or a wide range of PCs could be all the while surfing under one number because of contrasts in how systems are sorted out. Treats have a great deal of fans; however, they are less dependable than they used to be on the grounds that such a significant number of people erase them physically or naturally by means of security and protection programming. A further inconvenience is that if you have readers who decide to take your content in feed form as opposed to see your blog in their web browser, your crowd is really bigger than this measurement speaks to. Sponsors, particularly, as to know what number of unique visitors your blog pulls in a given month, and If you are going to sell your blog, this metric is critical too.

Visits

An individual visitor could make a few visits to a blog. You can measure visits more dependably than you can unique visitors, yet to contrast results you have with agree on what establishes a visit. Visits are likewise here and there termed "visitor sessions." Depending on who you tune in to and which programming you use to measure, a session could be determined in a few different ways. One mainstream approach to characterize a session is as a solid stream of page views after a specific time of inertia. If somebody visits two pages ten minutes separated, is that two-page views in a single session or two visits? Numerous website proprietors observe normal session length as an approach to determine to what extent people spend on their site. As websites become less about downloading pages and spotlight more on interactivity inside a page, session length is gaining fascination. The more drawn out visitors spend taking a gander at your content the better, since it implies they were progressively connected with and as indicated by media types, gaining greater partiality with your image.

Page Views

Page views are the absolute number of pages read in a web browser. Most bloggers like to realize what number of page views they pull in on a day by day and a month to month premise. In addition to the absolute page views, you should screen the proportion of pages viewed per visitor. It is ideal to have a high number of pages viewed and for the normal visitor to read more than one page. Each article you compose will get its very own page views, and by contrasting individual page forgets about you can work which articles are gaining the most consideration, giving you an idea what content your crowd finds generally intriguing.

Hits

Hit checks measure the number of requests sent for a file to the server. This is a dated and to a great extent unhelpful metric in light of the fact that each request for any file is counted. Despite the fact that it sounds valuable, in established truth it gives you noteworthy information. If you have a page containing four pictures, one request for that page is counted as five hits. To build your hits, you can add pictures to the page! Because of the deceptive idea of the metric, barely any people use it truly, and the term hits is regularly inaccurately utilized in discussion and the media when what they really mean is to portray traffic all in all, or explicitly visits or page views.

Subscribers

Bloggers can shift from being impassive about endorser counts to being fixated on them. For what reason are subscribers so important? Counting a blog's subscribers gives a decent sign of how mainstream it truly is on the grounds that subscribers are the people who need to read your content long haul and have joined to receive refreshes so they never miss one. These are your dedicated readers, the people you can ideally count on to return over and over. While the metrics referenced before are important, and they are customary measures for any website, subscribers are basic to blogs. A visit could be an individual showing up, not finding what they need, and leaving never to return. A supporter has made a little pledge to you and exhibits you are giving something valuable and convincing. Subscribers are normally part into RSS subscribers and email subscribers; despite the fact that, the lines are obscuring.

RSS Subscribers

RSS subscribers are the people who utilize your feed to read articles. They utilize a feed reader (service or programming application) to destroy down updates to your feed and may never really visit your blog. The most well-known feed-measurement service is FeedBurner.com, and along these lines, most bloggers rely on that service to think about progress against one another. Both Bloglines and Google give a count of readers utilizing their feedreader services, however just FeedBurner gives a count over every one of them. Despite the fact that about all bloggers rely on FeedBurner, even the organization would concede that counting feed readers isn't a precise science. Numbers vary each day, and glitches can make it appear as though you have lost or picked up readers arbitrarily. The best idea is to utilize the count as an advancement direct and not a careful count of individuals.

Email Subscribers

In addition to RSS readers, numerous bloggers distribute their content over email. There are services accessible to enable you to take your RSS feed and convey email refreshes naturally, and afterward there are master email-newsletter publishing services, for example, Aweber.com that enable you to make messages or import your content.

A favorable position that utilizing email records has over utilizing RSS is that when a visitor buys in you get his email address. A rundown of email tends to be a dependable pointer of what number of individuals you have bought in.

Comments, Feedback, and Interaction

As much as we as a whole need readers, when a blog is really captivating you will draw in comments. Comments show that your visitors need to interact with you. They enable you to build a feeling of network, further promising readers to return over and over.

Comments

You can start by counting the number of comments you receive in the wake of evacuating garbage and spam comments. If overall each article draws in ten comments, you realize you have made an improvement over when your blog increased just a couple. There are two types of posts you may especially need to receive: great feedback and thought about posts. If the main remark you receive is, "You suck," you probably won't be very as glad about those ten comments as back when you received two "pleasant post" comments per article!

Numerous bloggers additionally judge quality similarly as important as amount since it is so natural to simply post any old junk into the remark region, and people do just to get their very own notice website, however when somebody requires significant investment and care to make a mindful remark it tends to be considerably more fulfilling.

Feedback

Clearly, in addition to comments, people will utilize your contact form and email to connect with you. A significant number of my best articles have been roused by reader questions, and it is important to us all to receive feedback, good and terrible, so we know where we are turning out badly and what we are doing well.

Interaction

Past comments and emails, there are numerous ways that readers can take an interest on a blog. Participating in your blog may incorporate reactions to surveys, rivalry passages, and different invitations to take action. By and large, if people do in enormous numbers what you ask, at that point you have a connected with crowd!

Links

Links are the cash of the World Wide Web. The number of incoming links to your blog can be a pointer of how well you are connecting with different bloggers. Incoming links are good for a blog as a rule in view of the incoming traffic that tails them, yet in addition since they are a central point in climbing the rankings in search engines. They can be observed in a number of ways.

Trackbacks

If another blogger links to your article you can be advised utilizing an exceptional remark called a Trackback, which shows up linking back to the first blogger with a little statement of the content utilized. Despite the fact that a few bloggers detest them because of spammers exploiting the free connection back, blogs use them to promote discussions and as notice of what others are expounding on you.

Search Engines

To discover who is linking to you, type link: DomainName into Google. You can get a good snappy image of the incoming links that that search engine has recorded for your blog. There are additionally browser modules and simple to-utilize web services that will show you something very similar.

Referral Stats

Most insights bundles offer the capacity to follow where your readers originate from to get to your blog. This shows you the things they are searching search engines for yet, additionally the sites that are linking up.

Search-Engine Results

Getting to the highest point of a search-engine outcome for a specific expression can be the pass to a surge of traffic and appreciation from your friends. A few people take this to the degree of a game, considering it to be a game or rivalry, though others make a whole profession out of it since some search results merit a lot of money if you have something important to sell.

Chapter Five

Niche Blogging

One of the most important choices that bloggers needing to build a gainful blog need to make is the thing that their blog will be about. In this part we acquaint you with the idea of niche blogging and give you a few inquiries to pose to yourself when you are thinking about what topic to focus your blog upon. The majority of bloggers beginning in blogging do as such by making a personal blog. These blogs are, from numerous points of view, an expansion of the life of the blogger and usually spread a wide array of interests, going from life encounters to perceptions on work, leisure activities, connections, and passions. Personal blogs can be a ton of fun and are an extraordinary spot to learn about the rudiments of blogging; be that as it may, having a blog focus upon such an assortment of topics and diving into your personal life doesn't always make good marketing prudence.

I began with a personal blog that covered everything from spirituality and church to photography to blogging (and that's just the beginning), and however the blog became very well known, following year and a half of running it, I began to see a number of things that made me think about another methodology:

- Some readers got disillusioned with the blog — My blog had a number of primary topics and various readers reverberated distinctively with everyone. A couple of readers shared all of my assorted interests; in any case, most went to my blog to read about only one part of my life. At the point when I focused on a topic they were not interested in, they either disregarded the post or, on occasion, even pushed back. At last, a number of normal steadfast readers got disillusioned with my diverse way to deal with blogging and quit any pretense of reading me out and out.

- I began to feel remorseful about blogging on specific topics — Knowing that a considerable lot of my readers were disillusioned by my dispersed way to deal with blogging, I began to feel increasingly more blameworthy about posting on specific topics and began to dread the pushback that I realized I would get when posting on things that I was interested in, yet that a few readers were tired of reading about. Thus, I posted on topics that I was less interested in to pacify readers and overlooked different topics that I'd preferably have covered.

Reasons Why Niche Blogs Are Successful

Despite the fact that it isn't difficult to build a successful blog by blogging on a wide array of topics, the majority of gainful blogs that I've watched focus on a defined niche. Take a gander at the top blogs that you read normally, and you'll find that the majority of them have a defined niche. A few niches are wider than others, however in almost all cases they've cut out a niche for themselves. There are numerous reasons why choosing a niche is important for building a successful blog. We should investigate a couple of them:

- Loyal readers — Niche blogs will in general develop a dedicated readership since readers realize that when they sign into a blog, they'll get applicable information on topics that they have an enthusiasm for, as opposed to arbitrary posts on topics that they want to read.

- Community — People like to gather with others like them. Commonly when you develop a blog focusing on a solitary topic, you find that a gathering of similarly invested people will gather around it not simply to read what you need to state, yet to interact with other people who share their passions and interests.

- Specialist creators — Authors of niche blogs have the opportunity to focus upon a topic without feeling remorseful about doing as such. This can prompt an expansion in the amount, quality, and profundity of articles.

- Brand, credibility, and profile — Blogging reliably on one single topic expands the odds of that blog (and its blogger) being viewed as a sound, confided in wellspring of information around there. Work this effectively and you can turn into the "go-to" individual in your niche and become known as a pro or master in your field. The stream on advantages of this is colossal if you have a product or service of your own to sell. Rather than you expecting to proceed to search for clients, you'll find that people begin to search you out because of your skill.

- Contextual advertising — Contextual advertisement networks like AdSense will in general work best on sites that are firmly focused. They serve more focused on and important ads when an entire site is on a defined topic — which thusly improves the probability of those ads being clicked by readers.

- Ability to sell products — When you comprehend a niche well and draw in a group of people around it, you can make and sell products sure they have an anxious market and will be bought

- Direct advertising deals — Niche blogs are increasingly alluring to private promoters or patrons, who are searching for content to put their ads on that is important and firmly adjusted to their product or service.

- Search engine advancement — Google and other search engines will in general support sites with a well-defined topic with pages that identify with each other.

- More posts — I find that I post more if I have five blogs on five topics as opposed to one blog on five topics. There is just so a lot of you can compose on a blog every day without overpowering your readership.

- Leverage to venture into neighboring niches — One advantage of turning out to be well-known in an exceptionally focused niche is that you can situate yourself to springboard into a neighboring or larger one.

- Higher transformation — If your blog's plan of action is to sell something to your readers, it is to further your potential benefit to have a blog that has a readership with interests that are profoundly lined up with your own focus. Attempting to be all things to all people is a snare that a few bloggers fall into. Inspired by a paranoid fear of losing readers, they allow their content to get unfocused and off topic. Despite the fact that this may help build readership with regards to selling a product, your change rate will be altogether diminished in light of the fact that a lower level of readers will be really interested in your more focused on product.

Niche blogging gets progressively qualified possibilities. Choosing a niche for your blog empowers you, your bloggers, and your readers to turn out to be progressively focused and will empower you to grow a readership and adapt it all the more adequately.

How to Select a Profitable Niche Topic for Your Blog

Defining your niche is important If you need to build a successful blog; however how would you choose one?

Following is a progression of questions that we suggest you ask yourself as you make this important decision. We've incorporated some down to earth practices with each question to assist you with handling them all the more viably.

Is the Niche Growing or Shrinking?

The prevalence of various topics rises and falls after some time. Ideally you would need to choose a topic when it is on the ascent as opposed to when it is in decay. This isn't anything but difficult to do, obviously, however foresee the following enormous thing that people will be searching for and you could be onto a champ. Start being vigilant for what people are into. I continually ask myself, "What will people be searching the Web for in 6 to a year, and how might I position myself to be the site that they find when they do?" Keep an eye on what people are into, what the most recent patterns are, what occasions are coming up, and what product dispatches are not too far off. Do this on the web, yet in addition watch out for TV, magazines, the papers, and even the discussions you have with friends. Despite the fact that it isn't basic to be first to start a blog on a topic, it absolutely is early.

What's the Competition?

One of the snares that a few bloggers get sucked into while choosing a topic is to go for the most mainstream topics with no respect for the competition, they may face in those business sectors.

Will You Have Enough Content?

One of the key highlights of successful blogs is that they can keep on coming up with crisp content on their topic for extensive stretches of time. Then again, something that kills numerous blogs is that their creators come up short on things to state.

Addressing the question with respect to whether there is sufficient content ought to be done on two levels:

- Do you include enough content inside you as a creator? This really returns to the question we got some information about your enthusiasm, interests, and vitality for the topic (so I'll leave it at that).

- Do you approach enough different wellsprings of content and motivation? There are many Web-based instruments around nowadays that can help you in coming up with content. A few spots to look at your topic to perceive what news is about incorporate Google News, Digg, Popurls (Figure 2-1), StumbleUpon, and Reddit. Do a search for words in your proposed niche and you will rapidly perceive what amount is being expounded on them in predominant press and on different blogs.

Is the Niche Able to Be Monetized?

If you are interested in earning an income from blogging, you have to factor in some examination of whether the topic you've picked has any conspicuous potential income streams. There are a plethora ways to earn money from blogs (we acquaint you with a considerable lot of them later); be that as it may, the issue is that few out of every odd topic will be appropriate for each potential income stream.

For instance, logical advertisement programs like AdSense and Chitika work really well for certain topics, however, earn scarcely anything from others. Essentially, a few blogs do fantastically out of offshoot programs, some are more qualified to selling advertising straightforwardly to sponsors, and others are more qualified to impression-based ads. It very well may be hard to tell how well unique income streams will work on a blog before you actually start it and start to test. Notwithstanding, the all the more burrowing around and research you do before starting out, the better prepared you will be to decide on which niche topic to choose.

Choose a Niche

Now, it's time to choose a topic for your blog. It is exceptionally far-fetched that you'll find the ideal topic on all of the fronts talked about before. Despite the fact that it'd be incredible to find a topic that you're enthusiastic about that simply happens to have enormous interest, no competition, and heaps of worthwhile income streams, actually most topics that you concoct will have at any rate one weakness to them.

Try not to let this get you down; there comes a time when you simply need to make a decision and start blogging in light of the fact that the most ideal approach to find the solutions to a significant number of the questions in this part is to start a blog and see what you learn. The key is monitoring what the weakness is with the goal that you can work to beat it.

Tools to Aid You to Choose a Niche for Your Blog

Numerous tools have been developed that are useful for bloggers during the time spent choosing a niche topic for their blog. The following tools can be utilized in this research stage:

AdWords Keyword Tool — Sign up as a publicist with Google AdWords and you gain admittance to a number of valuable tools that you can use without actually expecting to utilize AdWords to promote. One especially valuable tool is the Keyword Tool

(https://adwords.google.com/select/KeywordTool),
which you should be signed in to utilize. This allows you
to type in a keyword (or state) and will give you an
indication of what number of people searched for that
word in the previous month just as tell you what number
of sponsors are competing for that word in AdWords.
This gives you an indication of the notoriety of the niche
and whether there is potential income in it. This tool will
likewise give you different keywords that identify with
the ones you enter, which is additionally helpful to know.

- Google Trends — Google has a free tool called
  Google Trends tool which can be found at
  www.google.com/patterns that is valuable for
  taking a gander at search volume on Google for
  various search terms. Despite the fact that it won't
  give you explicit search numbers and doesn't
  deliver results for each term (it tracks only the
  most well-known ones), it is valuable for
  working out whether a niche is developing or
  contracting and it allows you to contrast two
  distinct terms with give you how enormous one
  is in contrast with another.

- Google Blog Search — Google's Blog Search will assist you with getting an image of who else is blogging on a given topic.

- Wordtracker — Wordtracker is a famous keyword-research tool with a free preliminary that causes you to learn what number of people are searching for various words and what number of different sites are competing in those niches.

- Yahoo! Buzz — Yahoo! Buzz (http://buzz.yahoo.com/) is a synopsis of information on what people are searching for at the Yahoo! search engine.

Chapter Six

Setting Up Your Blog

So far we have seen what blogging is and being an expert blogger, and you have examined what you should expound on. We are set for a good start. Before you actually start blogging, however, you will need to set up your blog! In this part, we take a gander at your decisions when choosing which blog bundle to go with, what you have to consider while choosing, and what the most well-known mixes are.

After you have settled on what approach you think may suit you best, you have to actually feel free to set up your blog so it the two works and looks incredible. In view of these goals, we go step-by-step through setting up a hosted blog and a self-hosted blog.

Choosing the Right Blog for You

"Which blog platform should I use?" "Should I utilize a free hosted blog or get my very own domain?" "What are the advantages and disadvantages of going with one merchant over another?" "Might I be able to start out on a free blogging service and overhaul later?" These are only a portion of the regular questions that we get asked every day from novice bloggers attempting to choose which blogging platform or tool they ought to choose.

What Are Your Goals?

Presumably the most important activity when starting the way toward choosing a blog platform is to think about your desires for your blog. Obviously, complete newbies may battle a little with seeing the future of their blogging, however as well as could be expected, endeavor to address a portion of these questions:

- Is blogging a passing interest or something you will do long haul?

- What will be the principle reason for your blog?

- Is it for business, or only for personal delight?

- Might you need to show notices?

Obviously, there are numerous different questions you'll need to ask, yet the responses to these sorts of questions merit remembering as you research blog platforms. A few services are substantially more suited to the side interest blogger and others to progressively proficient blogging applications.

What Is Your Budget?

Similarly, as with most things in life, blog platforms accompany an assortment of value focuses. All hosted platforms offer differing levels of service, and self-installed programming fluctuates in cost from free to costly.

There are three principle things that you may pay for:

- The blog programming itself or level of service, one-off or continuous

- Monthly hosting for your blog

- Your domain name yearly reestablishment expense

There is likewise potentially an additional expense for hand craft and programming relying upon your budget and how genuine you are. A great many people start out with freely accessible structures and change them to suit their very own preferences and necessities. A few services, similar to Blogger and WordPress, offer an all-comprehensive service including the platform, a unique web address (in the format myblog.wordpress.com), and hosting for free.

TypePad offers a comparable all-incorporating on the web service with a month to month expense yet more customization choices. Others are downloadable programming that you need to install and have yourself. So, Despite the fact that they offer the platform for free, you at that point need to find and pay for your very own hosting and domain name and bolster it yourself.

Others still may charge for a permit for the platform, contingent upon what number of blogs you have and whether they will have a business, personal, instructive, or not-revenue driven use, and afterward you have to orchestrate and pay for your very own domain name and hosting on top.

How Technical Are You?

This is a critical factor to think about when choosing a blog platform. If you've never had any involvement with making a blog or website previously and are not a technologically minded individual, there are some blog platforms and setups that will be considerably more suited to your needs than if you know a couple of the rudiments, or if nothing else are eager to learn them. The other alternative, obviously, is to find somebody who is a geek to enable you to out (either paid or as a companion). An extraordinary aspect regarding blogging and the majority of the platforms is that there is a great common information out there and numerous discussions committed to helping people benefit from their picked platforms.

What Blog Platforms Are Others Using?

Despite the fact that your blog is your own individual decision and should fit with your very own style, it merits checking out you to perceive what others, specifically people you know well, are utilizing. In the course of recent years various platforms have traveled every which way, and you need to presume this will keep on occurring in the future.

By a wide margin the most famous platforms right now for ace bloggers are WordPress (both self-hosted and the online service), TypePad, Blogger, and Movable Type. We have attempted different platforms, yet now chiefly use WordPress.

Hosted vs. Self-Hosted

As recently mentioned, there are two primary types of blogging platforms: programs you install and host yourself, and online services that handle everything for you. These are regularly alluded to as self-hosted blogs and hosted blogs.

Hosted Blog Platforms

This is the type of blog that numerous bloggers start out with, essentially in light of the fact that they are fast, easy, and can be free. Presumably the most popular of these systems with professional bloggers are TypePad, WordPress, and Blogger, with just TypePad having a month to month expense. These systems are "hosted" blog platforms since they "host" your blog without anyone else domain. After what is usually a really easy setup process, they will give you a web address (URL) that will usually be their very own mix URL and the name of your blog, for instance, http://problogger .wordpress.com. Despite the fact that this is the thing that you get as a default, you are currently regularly given the decision of paying a charge to utilize your very own domain. This is something well worth considering If you are not kidding about blogging. Preferences of Hosted Blog Platforms Using a hosted platform has numerous favorable circumstances.

The absolute most quick are recorded here:

- Cheap or free to run — Most hosted options are free.

- Easy and Quick to set up — Setting up of most types of blogs can be with a fundamental default layout inside minutes. The setup is usually simply an issue of filling in a couple of fields with your options and choosing a layout structure. They are ideal If you know nothing or almost no about the innovative side of blogging. You'll see more on this later.

- Simple to run — Once you're through the easy setup process, hosted blogs are usually really easy to run. You will clearly need to learn a few rudiments, yet nowadays most blog platforms accompany user-friendly includes. Posting is as basic as filling in a couple of content boxes and clicking Publish.

- Updated automatically — If the blog platform transforms, it will automatically overhaul for you. Rather than transferring new programming onto a server, these updates happen substantially more flawlessly.

- Search engines and traffic — One of the benefits of many hosted blog platforms is that they are hosted and connected from sites that already pull in search engine consideration and traffic. A portion of this "focuses on" on your blog, giving it a little lift.

Disadvantages of Hosted Blog Platforms

Despite the fact that there are a few advantages to having a hosted blog, there are always drawbacks:

- Less configurable — With an online service, the main design options you have accessible are those the service allows you. This could conceivably be an issue for you, however much of the time you have less options with a hosted service.

- Default plan confinements — This can be valid for standalone blogging systems; however, many hosted blogs wind up looking fundamentally the same as each other. This is on the grounds that the default layouts get utilized again and again, and hosted platforms don't give you unlimited authority over your look and feel.

- Less possession — Another objection I hear normally from hosted-blog proprietors is that they are disappointed by not having extreme control and responsibility for blog. Despite the fact that they do claim the content, the URL isn't technically their very own and they are to some degree helpless before their platform in terms of whether their blog is working.

- Generic URL — There are some successful blogs on hosted platforms, however most bloggers accept that having your very own URL is substantially more professional if you are utilizing your blog in a professional manner

- Upgrading or moving challenges — One of the issues of starting out with a hosted platform is that, if there comes a day when you need to move, you have some work cut out for you in holding your crowd and traffic.

- Non-business or lacking adaptation options — Most adaptation options expect you have total possession and control of your blog site, and some hosted arrangements prohibit you to make a blog for business reasons.

Who Might Use Hosted Blog Platforms?

If you simply need a blog and don't think much about having your own unique domain and you are not very interested in tweaking your blog or getting all the best in class highlights, hosted options are a totally legitimate decision. Truth be told, it merits remembering that however some may laugh at hosted blog platforms and state that genuine bloggers don't utilize them, there are some popular bloggers who have utilized them successfully or began that way. For instance, three of my preferred blogs cut their teeth on hosted services: Scott Adams and Robert Scoble, started out with hosted blogs, and Seth Godin, still uses TypePad right up 'til the present time (http://sethgodin.typepad.com/).

Standalone Blog Platforms

The other type of blog platform is the place you download, install, and host the product yourself. This is the thing that Darren and I do with all of our blogs nowadays. You will see our blogs have their own domains, chrisg.com and problogger.net, and as I said previously, we both use WordPress all alone server spaces. Despite the fact that we are fully for people going the hosted course, you do gain more power when you host your blog yourself. Obviously, this is a double-edged sword! Advantages of Self-Hosted Blog Platforms As mentioned previously, both hosted and self-installed platforms have their own preferences and disadvantages. Here are simply the advantages hosted blogs:

- Full control — Depending upon your ability with the innovation and web plan, standalone blogs generally are entirely versatile. Despite the fact that I am totally content with the geekier parts of blogs, I am not the best originator, so I will in general incline toward others for feel. There are architects out there who figure out how to make unbelievably different and smart plans for blogs and accommodate download both free and paid topics, so it should be conceivable to make your blog look phenomenal.

- Adaptability — One of the things I appreciate about WordPress is the huge range of developers who are coming up with all way of "modules," which broaden the ability of the essential WordPress installation. A considerable lot of the other standalone platforms have networks of developers creating comparable additional items.

- Free platforms — Although you wind up paying for your domain name and hosting, systems like these are usually free to run. Some have permit expenses, yet a large portion of the popular ones are free to utilize.

- URL — Having your very own domain name is extraordinary for some reasons. For one, it's easier to recall; second, it's increasingly professional; and third, it is all the more effectively brandable. Disadvantages of Self-Hosted Blog Platforms Although I have blogs set up along these lines, it could be an inappropriate decision for you for the following reasons:

- Complicated setup — Again, this relies on your specialized capacities, yet when you move into standalone platforms the multifaceted nature of setup will in general increment. At any rate it includes organizing hosting and a domain name. There is an abundance of network bolster accessible, however for some, it is still an overwhelming possibility. One approach to improve the procedure is to find a web host that gives "a single tick installs" of popular bundles. Perceive how much easier this makes things later in this section.

- Cost — Although the blog platform itself may be free, you have to factor in the progressing expenses of having your own domain name (a yearly charge in addition to a coincidental enrollment expense) and hosting expenses (month to month or yearly). There are numerous extraordinary arrangements out on these, so it need not cost the world, however If your blog gets a great deal of traffic, the expenses can go up, and you should consider going onto a progressively professional, and accordingly, increasingly costly arrangement.

- Updates — Most blog platforms experience changes and forms after some time. Refreshing starting with one then onto the next can be entangled if you don't recognize what you're doing.

- Hosting issues — I mentioned in the cons of the hosted platforms that you possess "less control" over your blog and are at the impulse of your platform's.

Choosing a Domain Name

Having your own domain name is attractive for professional bloggers for a few reasons. For starters, if you need to build credibility and a feeling of professionalism around your blog, a domain can help. Also, a carefully chosen domain name can improve the branding and memorability of a product, service, business, or even individual. Domain buys give the special reward of email addresses with a similar domain (adding to both professionalism and branding) and can to a degree upgrade your search engine positioning.

Factors to Consider When Selecting a Domain Name

Similarly, as there are numerous factors to consider in choosing the name of your kid, business, or pet, there are numerous ramifications of choosing names for a website. What follows is a rundown of factors to remember as you make the decision. Remember that there are numerous hypotheses about what is good and bad here and that, despite all the guidelines that people have, there are some successful sites that overlook them all! Likewise, worth remembering is that personal taste comes into decisions like this; what appears to be a good name to you will regularly mean various things to various people.

In view of those disclaimers, investigate a couple of zones to consider:

- What are your goals and objectives? We regularly return to this point since where you are going is such an important piece of thinking about the long-haul vision that you have for your blog. Might you need to eventually sell it?

- What is the topic of the blog? A conspicuous starting point, maybe, yet worth considering. Names can mirror the blog's topic or niche.

- Why are you blogging? For you, is blogging about having a pastime? Is it about building your profile/mastery? Is it about earning an income by means of ads? Is it to help a current business ?

- What style will it be? Will you blog alone, or will there be numerous creators? What length of posts will it have?

- What voice and tone will it be written in? Will it be conversational, newsy, tirades, professional, or comical?

- Who is the target group? Would you like to speak to businesses, youngsters, cool people, Moms, local people, nerds ?

- What is the wellspring of traffic? Domains can create "type in" traffic; this is when people surmise at or remember a domain name and type it in to the URL bar as opposed to search for it. This is the reason domains like business.com and sex.com sell for millions. Then again, domains can have an effect on search engines if the keywords are available in the name.

- Branding — Many discourses on domain name decisions talk about choosing between a domain name with keywords in it and domain names that are increasingly brandable or conventional. It merits expressing in advance that it is conceivable to accomplish both, yet I would organize memorability and branding over keywords. One model that rings a bell is Engadget. com, which has become an important and well-marked name that additionally figures out how to fuse the keyword "device".

- Future bearings — Another factor to think about that is identified with characterizing your goals and objectives is to think about what your blog may resemble in the future. I've seen bloggers change their interests after some time and be left with barely focused domains or need to grow from having a blog to a bigger network. Obviously, you can get another domain, yet it is less befuddling and easier to showcase if you get it directly from the word "go." Another "future factor" to consider is what number of blogs you're thinking of starting on your domain. Investigate About.com for a case of how it's conceivable to have one domain with numerous blogs running off it.

In conclusion on the "future front" — don't pick a name that you think may date rapidly. Picking a name that is time-explicit in any capacity may find you searching for another domain when it is never again important at some future time:

- Name length and spellings — Opinions on what the ideal length of a domain name change. Technically, you can have really long names and still be substantial, however it is generally acknowledged that short ones are better. You need your crowd to have the option to rapidly and effectively state, spell, and remember your domain. The more drawn out and harder it is to articulate or spell, the more uncertain you will get good word of mouth.

- Domain endings — Along with the discussions over domain name length come a wide range of assessments over what is ideal to have toward the finish of your domain after the "speck." These letters (that is, .com, .net, .org, etc.) are technically called the Top-Level Domains (TLDs) and are separated into two types. First there are country code TLDs, and second there are "conventional" TLDs that imply various types of organizations (in principle, in any event). There is an assortment of ways to deal with choosing which TLD to go for, however except if you are focusing on a particular country (for instance, .fr for France) or have a specific legitimate or organizational structure to work inside (for instance, .edu for instruction), when all is said in done you should go after .com first, at that point go after the others, for example, .org or .net.

- Hyphens — Another continuous discussion about domain names is over the estimation of hyphenated names. For instance, a hyphenated adaptation of Darren's blog may be Pro-

Blogger.net. There are two main reasons that a few people incline toward hyphenated names:

- Availability — One of the main reasons for going with hyphens is that all the good names are taken (or possibly it can appear along these lines). Addition of hyphens to names gives more options.

- SEO — Hyphens are said by some to recognize keywords to search engines all the more obviously.

Be that as it may, I have questions regarding how successful this is in the wider plan of things. Obviously, for each positive there is a negative, and the contentions against hyphens incorporate the following:

- Memorability — Adding hyphens can make it precarious for readers to remember your name.

- Difficult to convey — Have you at any point attempted to tell somebody a domain name with a hyphen between each word? It very well may be a significant irritating procedure.

- Increased edge for blunder — The more characters in your domain name, the more possibility of a mixed-up keystroke.

- Cheap and awful factor — There is an observation that hyphens are spammy. I personally don't mind a domain with one or perhaps two hyphens most extreme, however domains-that-have-parts of hyphens-turn-me-off. There are numerous bloggers who have been turned down when requesting links due to their spammy looking domains, so my recommendation is to keep away from them

- Numbers — Another choice to think about when choosing a domain on a topic that is very packed is to remember a number for it. Indeed, this expands your odds of finding a domain with your keyword in it yet could add to perplexity (do you spell out the number or not?).

- Keeping it lawful — Think intensely about the lawful ramifications of the words you use in your domain name and maintain a strategic distance from trademarked names especially. I am aware of two or three cases where bloggers were constrained into making changes a very long time into new blogs as a result of legitimate dangers.

- The "blog" word — One allurement for some, bloggers is to utilize the word "blog" in the name and URL of their blog. I did this with the dslrblog.com domain. This has the upside of opening up new options for domain names, however, confines the domain to being perpetually utilized as a blog and that's it.

- Secure multiple domains — One suggestion that many experienced webmasters prescribe is making certain that you secure other comparable domain names to the one you eventually choose. For instance, if you choose a .com domain name it may merit getting the .net and .org ones if you can, or maybe in any event, getting plurals or other sensible, comparable ones. This isn't basic yet may assist you with securing your niche in certain conditions.

- Opinions of others — Before you buy that domain you've been eyeing; it may be beneficial to run it by a couple of confided in friends (who won't run off and buy it for themselves). It's astounding how focused you can become on finding the correct name and how that can cloud your judgment. It's additionally fascinating to perceive how a name may sound to an individual of an alternate culture. Words mean various things in various pieces of the world, and it could assist you with evading a humiliating misstep or only a dorky blog name.

- Previously utilized domain names — It merits verifying whether a domain has been recently enrolled. Spammers regularly buy domain names and afterward abandon them later once they've utilized them. This can leave these domains restricted by Google, which may get you off to an entirely poor start. Then again, people abandon flawlessly real sites all the time, and a terminated domain could be a deal when you consider there may already be links highlighting it, or existing traffic.

Chapter Seven

Blog Design Considerations

A great deal of your blog's initial effect will be from your design. In the first segment, we just picked a layout off the rack, however you will have substantially more success if you spend a little idea and exertion on furnishing your blog with the ideal look. Numerous people are put off by terrible design before reading even a solitary word of content. A good design can really set off your content, make your blog show up more thought about and professional, which can assist you with getting those significant subscribers. Before choosing a design for a blog you have to choose a few things:

- What is your blog objective? Is it true that you are focusing on AdSense benefit, to sell products, acclaim? AdSense templates will in general free up more space for advertising, though if distinction is your objective you will need a huge sidebar region for your "About Me" box.

- Who is your audience? Out of control? No nonsense? Forefront? If your intended interest group is the meeting room, you will require a more traditional design than if your audience is for the most part made up of designers. This will impact your realistic and shading decisions.

- What explicit capacities does the site need? Certain templates have a larger number of capacities than others. Some are made to fulfill a specific reason, for example, templates for photograph bloggers. Do you need header tabs? Randomized masthead pictures? Adaptable square statements? Here are some standard highlights you have to consider and allow space for:

    - Contact subtleties

    - About or bio details/photograph

- Advertising

- Archives by classes

- Archives by date

- Logo

- Subscription catches

- Newsletter information exchange

- Search highlight

- Blog roll

- Recent posts list

- Links to more established key posts

A Word on Color

As everyone knows, shading influences state of mind. What do you need the state of mind of your blog to be? You will surely get an alternate outcome with a pink blog than a dark one. Hues mean something just as look decent. You know the works of art:

- Red = enthusiasm, blood, outrage

- Blue = moderate, business

- Green = nature, go

- Gray = formal, staid Carefully think about what feel you need to extend and what potential implications your shading plan ought to be related with.

Chapter Eight

Blog Writing

Much has been composed on what makes a blog successful, however all specialists agree that integral to all extraordinary blogs is one element: incredible content. The cry, "Content is top dog," has resounded through the blogosphere for quite a long time; despite the fact that I think the term disregards different parts of what makes a blog successful, content is a key element of a successful blog.

What Is Good Content?

Characterizing good content is an abstract exercise (maybe along these lines to characterizing a good book or a good film). Good content will shift from person to person contingent on their needs, the topic they are discussing, and maybe even a person's morals. Not exclusively will bloggers themselves each have an alternate view on what good content is, yet readers tend to likewise. I realize that each time I request feedback about what I expound on ProBlogger, I get a genuine range of reactions. Having said this, there are a few things that can be said about good content, and in this section, we endeavor to unload some of them. At most focuses en route there will be debate, yet hopefully you will have the option to blend and match the elements and distinguish what works for you. So, with no progressively early on comments, how about we get into it with the principal element of composing quality content.

Handiness and Uniqueness

Let me start our investigation of good content with a genuinely self-evident, yet important, articulation: For a blog to be successful, your content should be helpful and unique to your readers. It isn't advanced science, yet two questions that bloggers need to continually ask themselves are, "Is my blog valuable?" and, "How is it not the same as different blogs?" Back in the days when I considered showcasing, I remember sitting in lecture after lecture getting increasingly more disappointed as I tuned in to my lecturer's drum into us something very similar time after time. Despite the fact that they said it in various ways, the exercise that they imparted was to a great extent the equivalent in each example and came down to this: "Start with the client — find out what they need and give it to them." This is a good exercise for bloggers too. I would likewise suggest that you start with yourself as a blogger and blog out of your own passions, encounters, and information, however it is fundamental that you know about your reader and that you make content that will add something to their lives. Give them something helpful and unique.

What Is Useful Content?

Helpful content to me is unique in relation to what it is to you, yet could be any of the following:

- Entertainment — Increasingly, blogs are being utilized as stimulation. People are going to them for giggles, tattle, and fun discussion.

- Education — Some blog readers are basically interested in learning something about a given topic.

- Information — Many successful blogs are based on the thirst that some must be informed on an issue, product, or topic.

- Debate — Some blog readers need a spot that they can have a good old exchange, debate, or even a battle about an issue.

- News — Many blog readers simply need to be stayed up with the latest with the most recent news on a topic.

- Community — People want to have a place. Numerous successful blogs tap into this and are tied in with interfacing people interested in investigating a topic. Regularly the topic is optional to the real relationship based on the blog.

- Each blog can possibly be helpful in an alternate manner, and it would presumably be indiscreet to start a blog that attempted to be all of these things without a moment's delay (Although numerous blogs do an assortment of these things immediately).

Research Your Readership

The best guidance that I could give on developing valuable content is to research your readership (or potential readership). If you already have a blog, do this by looking over your readers (either formally or informally) or by requesting feedback. I routinely approach my readers for questions, and a lot of what I compose rises legitimately from these inquiries. Another fast tip for finding what questions your readers are asking is to check the referral measurements of your blog to perceive what words people are composing into search engines (SEs) to find your blog.

An extraordinary little tool for this is Google Webmaster Tools, which tracks how people land at your blog and recognizes questions being asked by your readers in search engines. If you don't have a blog already, you'll have to work somewhat harder to research your potential readers. Review friends follow the comments areas of different blogs on your topic to perceive what readers are asking there and look in gatherings and online discourse bunches that spread your topics, where there is usually a great deal of question asking going on. As you do this, you'll start to put your finger on what people need and what you may have the option to give to address these issues.

Unique Content

Another factor to think about when thinking about good content is its uniqueness. Technorati tells us that a blog is being made each second, and that there are tens of millions of blogs in presence today. This presents bloggers with the challenge of building a blog that stands apart from the group.

I see blogs each day that give "helpful" content however that have no readers essentially in light of the fact that people are finding that information in different spots.

Distinguish Yourself

New bloggers attempting to break into a niche where others are already blogging should surf through different blogs and websites in that niche and do some examination on what kind of content those blogs and websites are creating. In many niches, you'll find that sites are all displaying fundamentally the same as information in essentially a similar voice, tone, and style. As another blogger on the topic, you have a decision: You can either reproduce what they are doing and attempt to improve (troublesome in light of the fact that they will already have faithful readers, and except if you're brilliant at it you're probably not going to change over these readers over to you), or you can distinguish yourself somehow or another from what others are doing.

This may mean focusing on a marginally unique topic (maybe a sub-niche) yet could likewise mean writing in an unmistakable voice. (Investigate Manolo's Shoe Blog for a case of a blogger who has grown a faction audience by writing about an odd mix of topics as an unknown blogger writing as an outsider looking in.) It may likewise mean writing in an alternate sort of posts. (That is, if every other person is writing newsy posts, you may jump at the chance to compose more assessment type posts.) Bring together the elements of helpful and unique in your content, and you will be one step more like a successful blog.

Writing Tips for Bloggers

Writing for the Web — and all the more especially on blogs — is altogether different than writing in different mediums. In this segment, we investigate some functional tips for writing adequately as a blogger.

Searchable Content

Web clients are known for not remaining on web pages long and for skimming through content as opposed to reading it word for word. This is considerably more the situation when readers read through their RSS feeds. As opposed to reading each word on a web page, web clients examine pages for information, searching for keywords, phrases, and obvious signs.

As a result, it is important to learn how to compose content that is searchable. Here are a couple of tips and procedures you can use for working with your filtering readers rather than against them:

- Lists — This will be nothing unexpected to ProBlogger readers — I'm really enthusiastic about records and my details give me it's my posts with bulleted or numbered records in them that get linked to and read much more than similar-length posts written in an article style.

- Formatting — Use intense, CAPITALS, italics, underlining, and other formatting procedures to emphasize points. Don't go over the edge, since you run the danger of baffling your reader. Do be cautious with underlining on the grounds that it is likewise commonly used to demonstrate that text is a link. Likewise consider changing text dimension, shading, and style to draw your readers' eyes to your main points.

- Headings and subheadings — Using headings halfway through posts assists with post structure, yet headings likewise are extraordinary for drawing your readers' eyes down the page and helping them find important points and the elements of your article that will most interest them.

- Pictures — Clever utilization of pictures in your posts can catch eye, emphasize points, and draw people down into your post. In a to a great extent text-driven medium, pictures will give your post visual points of interest. I've tried how readers respond to pictures in posts, and pictures are especially successful at the highest point of posts to get people reading and advantageous to break up the text in longer posts and to draw the eye to activity things.

- Borders/square statements — Boxes around statements and key points can similarly get the attention of readers.

- Space — Don't feel you need to fill up every last bit of your screen; rather, make spaces since they help readers not to feel overpowered and, once more, will in general draw readers' eyes to what is inside such spaces.

- Short passages — Web clients will in general become mixed up in enormous squares of text; break text into smaller nibbles, and you'll find people keep on reading a post longer.

- Don't bury your points — Make your main points as clear as possible and get your main point crosswise over in the initial scarcely any sentences instead of burying it in your decision.

Utilizing Titles Effectively on Blogs

Well-composed titles are important on numerous fronts, including the following:

- Grabbing attention in search engines — Go to Google and type in virtually any word you can consider, and you'll frequently find millions of results. Curiously, for most search results in Google (and other search engines) there is next to no for readers to pass by in choosing which result to tap on. There is a title, a short portion, and a URL. The most featured of these is the title, and I trust it is a vital aspect for getting search-engine referral visitors.

105

- Getting RSS readers' attention — In a fundamentally the same as way, titles can catch the eye of those following your blog by means of RSS feeds in news aggregators. News-aggregator readers will in general output the titles of posts for things of interest instead of reading full text, halting to read and visiting the posts that provoke their curiosity. A similar standard is valid in social bookmarking sites like Digg.com and Delicious.com, which can possibly send your site a large number of visitors put together exclusively with respect to the title of your post.

- Loyal readers — Good titles additionally sway the manner in which your unwavering readers interact with your blog. As I've already mentioned, web clients examine pages, and probably the most ideal ways to make them delay as they roll their eyes down your site is to catch their attention with a good title that interests them enough to hinder their mad web surfing and actually read a portion of the content that you've emptied time and vitality into.

- Search engine streamlining — Though there are numerous factors that add to how search engines rank a page of your blog, one of the most dominant onsite factors is the words that you use in the title of that page. Of course, most blogging platforms remember your title for the title labels of your post's page and the URL structure of that page; both of these factors add to that page's search-engine positioning. Add to this that different bloggers frequently utilize your title to link to you (an amazing thing), and your titles become an important factor in positioning well and creating traffic in search engines.

How to Utilize Titles Successfully

There are numerous procedures that successful bloggers use to draw attention to their posts with titles. There is no genuine set in stone, and likewise with numerous parts of blogging, what is a good title is abstract. At last the objective of your title is to get people to read the main line of your post. To do this, think about a portion of these systems:

- Keep it simple — Most research that I've seen about titles contends that the best titles are short, simple, and easy to comprehend. Despite the fact that breaking these standards can help grab attention (see the following thing) they can likewise befuddle, disappoint, and put a coated look at without flinching of potential readers. Shorter titles are likewise good for search engines; keep in search results in Google.

- Grab attention — Good titles set your posts separated from the messiness around them and draw readers into your post. Attention may be accomplished utilizing tactics of stun, huge cases, debate, or even disarray. Despite the fact that these tactics do work at getting people in, it ought to likewise be said that they can accomplish more harm than good if the remainder of your post doesn't satisfy the guarantees your title makes. By all methods attempt to grab attention, simply don't fool your readers into thinking you'll furnish them with something you can't give them.

- Meet a need — A powerful title draws people into reading more since they feel you have a comment that they have to hear. Files like del.icio.us illustrate exactly how compelling this is. Regularly the articles that get to the highest priority on the rundown are "the means by which to..." or "instructional exercise"- type articles that tell readers the best way to take care of an issue or need that they may have.

- Describe — Some readers are drawn into a post by an obscure title that doesn't tell them much about what they'll be reading, however the majority of readers need to know something about what they'll find if they read further. Titles ought to depict what readers will get in the main post. They don't have to give away everything in the post, however being unmistakable will help.

- Use keywords — As I mentioned prior, titles are a ground-breaking some portion of SEO. If you need to maximize their capacity, you have to consider utilizing the keywords that you need your post to be found within your title somehow or another. This, obviously, is challenging when you are endeavoring to keep it simple and to likewise grab attention and interest, however it very well may be done. Words toward the start of titles are believed to be more dominant than words toward the end with regards to SEO.

- Take as much time as necessary with the writing of post titles. Numerous bloggers empty a lot of exertion into writing drawing in and interesting posts, yet then simply slap any old title onto it without understanding that in doing so they may be guaranteeing that their post is never read. Treat your title as a smaller than usual commercial for your work. Take at any rate a couple of moments before hitting Publish to not just make sure your post is all together, however that your title will do all that it can to maximize the odds that people will draw in with what you need to state.

Opening Lines Matter

The reason for a post title is to get readers to read the principal line of your post. Be that as it may, to get people to read your full post, your opening lines are additionally significant. Readers will make a judgment about whether your full post merits reading dependent on how it starts, and they will keep reading if you prevail with regards to associating with them on one of a number of levels. Opening links should provoke curiosity and interest, feature a need that your reader has, show an advantage of reading on, and additionally make a type of guarantee to engage, inform, educate, or offer something of significant worth. You don't have to do all of these things in the opening sentence of each post you write, however if you need your readers to arrive at the base of your posts and to be convinced by what you write, you'll have to work hard at an opportune time at snaring them in some way or another.

Post Length — How Long Should a Blog Post Be?

The ideal length of a blog post has been fervently debated by bloggers for quite a long time, and there are a number of factors to think about when thinking about it, for example, the following:

- Reader attention length — It is really well archived that the run of the mill web reader has a short attention range with regards to reading content online. My very own examination concerning length of remain on blogs found that normal blog readers remain 96 seconds. That is a moment and a half to impart to your readers. As a result, numerous webmasters deliberately hold their content length down to a level that is readable in short grabs.

- SEO — There is a genuinely solid sentiment among those considered specialists in search engine improvement that both very short and amazingly long web pages are not positioned as profoundly as pages that are of a reasonable length. Obviously, nobody really realizes what number of words are ideal in the eyes of Google and its fellow search engines, however the general supposition is by all accounts that a page of in any event 250 words is most likely a reasonable length. Similarly, many prompt keeping pages under 1,000 words.

- Quantity of posts — One hypothesis that goes around is that shorter posts allow you to write more posts and that more posts are better for creating readership with RSS and in search engines. Despite the fact that I don't know their technique personally, some accept this is the thing that sites like Engadget and Gizmodo do with the high amount of short posts that make up the majority of their content.

- Topic/kind — The type of post that you're writing will frequently determine its length. For instance, when writing an audit of a product, you'll generally write a more extended post than when you write a news-related post where you link to something another person has composed.

- Comprehensive inclusion of the topic — Ultimately, this must be the main model that bloggers go with. Write enough to exhaustively cover your topic and afterward stop. Long posts for them are not an insightful move, yet nor are short ones that don't cover the topic well. My personal inclination is to mix up my post length from post to post. I attempt to write one long post for every day to give readers something substantial to bite on, yet I likewise mix in short newsy posts most days. Post Frequency — How Often Should a Blogger Post? One of the common suggestions that I see given to new bloggers is that they ought to write visit posts on their blog. This is good guidance, however as far as I can tell it's not exactly as simple as that. I think posting frequency is an issue that bloggers need to consider carefully on a number of fronts:

- Writer burnout — Every year, I do a 24-hour blogathon to fund-raise for a philanthropy. Despite the fact that I appreciate the procedure a lot, I find that it generally forgets about me very consumed — physically just as in my ability to write. This is an extraordinary model, yet it occurs if your posting frequency is too high over a continued period. The steady drive for high caliber and significant content is something that negatively affects a blogger. Post over and over again and the nature of your writing could suffer for it.

- Reader burnout — Too numerous posts can likewise forget about your readers consumed. I as of late approached ProBlogger readers for the reasons that they unsubscribe to blogs, and "such a large number of posts" was among the top reasons. I know from personal experience of reading blogs that if my news aggregator shows that there are in excess of 20 unread posts on a blog, I'm more averse to read each post in full and will unsubscribe from it If I can't keep up.

- Reader participation — Post over and over again, and you'll not give your readers enough space to have good discussions in the comments of your posts. Each time you post, you push ongoing articles further down the first page of your blog, making them more averse to be seen and reacted to by readers. Additionally, there are just such huge numbers of discussions that your readers can have without a moment's delay. Post too often every day and they'll feel overpowered and give up attempting to take part.

- Search engine and RSS referrals — One of the reasons to consider expanding your posting frequency is that the bigger the amounts of value content that you produce, the more open entryways you have into your blog by means of both search engines and your RSS feed. Despite the fact that you hazard baffling readers with high post levels, it generally leads to higher traffic.

- Blog topic — I'm a firm adherent that there is no "one size fits all" way to deal with posting frequency on blogs. One of the main reasons for this is various topics will in general loan themselves to various styles of blogging. For example, a blog like Engadget has a wide topic (purchaser hardware/contraptions). This topic covers a lot of subcategories and to do it equity it needs to post a high number of posts (at least 20 every day). Its readership knows this, and I speculate a lot of them need it, as they are attempting to stay aware of a wider industry. Device darlings are likewise regularly information junkies who are usually technically knowledgeable and ready to devour bigger measures of information. Different blogs with more tightly topics would not have the option to continue such a huge number of posts in light of the fact that there is just such a great amount to write about on some random day.

- Visitor type — I've already addressed this a bit (in saying device fans are frequently information junkies) however another way that your visitor type can affect posting frequency is the wellspring of the visitor. For instance, at ProBlogger.net I have a lot higher readership that comes by means of RSS subscribers and bookmarks than on my advanced camera blog, which is generally visited via search-engine clients and those coming from my email pamphlet. As a result, it isn't as pivotal that I keep my posting level down to a reasonable level on my photography blog, since it's not prone to affect numerous people. Truth be told, having more posts can be useful in light of the fact that it implies there are all the more arrival points for SE traffic.

- Post length — Another perception that numerous people make about the absolute most highly visited blogs is that while they post a lot more much of the time than different blogs, their post length is shorter, making the high number of everyday posts less irritating.

Chapter Nine

Types of Blog Posts

One of the traps that I see a few bloggers fall into is that their blogs regularly become very one-dimensional in terms of the type of posts they write. Mixing up the types of post that you write can mix it up and character to your blog, which will keep readers as time goes on. There are numerous types of posts that you may get a kick out of the chance to use; here are 20 to start exploring different avenues regarding:

- Instructional — Instructional posts tell people how to accomplish something. I find that posts that contain tips or that are instructional exercises generally are the ones that are among my generally popular. One of the main things that people search the Web for is to find help in overcoming a problem. Position yourself to answer these problems, and you can build a pleasant wellspring of traffic over the long haul.

- Informational — This is one of the more common blog post types, where a blogger basically gives information on a topic. It could be a definition post or a more drawn out clarification of some part of the niche that you're writing on. This is the essence of successful sites like Wikipedia.

- Reviews — Another highly searched-for term on the Web is "review." Every time I'm thinking about buying another product I head to Google and search for a review on it first. I realize that I'm not the only one. Reviews come in all shapes and measures and on virtually every product or service you can consider. Give your reasonable and smart opinion and approach readers for their opinion; reviews can be highly amazing posts that have a great life span.

- Lists — One of the simplest ways to write a post is to make a rundown. Posts with content like,

"The Top Ten ways to...," "7 Reasons why...," "5 Favorite...," or "53 slip-ups that bloggers make when..." are easy to write yet are usually popular with readers and can be successful at getting links from different bloggers.

- Interviews — Sometimes when you've run out of keen things to state it may be a good idea to let another person do the talking in an interview. This is a great way not exclusively to give your readers a significant master's opinion, yet to maybe even learn something about the topic you're writing. One tip in case you're moving toward people for an interview on your blog is don't overpower them with questions. A couple of good questions are bound to get you a reaction than a not insignificant rundown of ill-conceived ones.

- Case examines — Another popular type of post is the contextual investigation, where you walk readers through a case of something that you're writing about. These are valuable posts for readers since they are genuine circumstances and frequently have pragmatic tips related with them.

- Profiles — Profile posts are similar to contextual analyses however focus in on a specific person. Pick an interesting personality in your niche and do a little research on them to present to your readers. Point out how they've arrived at the position they are in and write about the qualities that they have that others in your niche may get a kick out of the chance to develop to be successful.

- Link posts — The "link post" is a most loved form of blogging for some bloggers and is just an issue of finding a quality post on another site or blog and linking ready. You would usually likewise incorporate a clarification of why you're linking up, a comment of your own interpretation of the topic, as well as a statement from the post. Including your very own comments makes these posts increasingly unique and valuable to your readers. The more unique content the better, yet don't be reluctant to ricochet off others along these lines. These link posts are ground-breaking since they not just give your readers something good to read, however they can get you saw and assist you with building associations with different bloggers.

- "Problem" posts — Another term that is regularly searched for in Google related to product names is the word "problem" or "problems" — that is, the place people are searching for help on a problem that they may have with something that they possess or are attempting to do. Problem posts are similar to review posts, however, focus more upon the negatives of a product or service. Don't write these pieces only for them, yet If you find a certifiable problem with something, a problem post can work for you.

- Comparison posts — Life is full of circumstances that expect you to make decisions between at least two options. Write a post differentiating two products, services, or approaches that outlines the positives and negatives of every decision. It could be said these are review posts however are somewhat wider in focus. I find that these posts do very well on a portion of my product blogs where people actually search for "X Product correlation with Y Product" or "X versus Y" in search engines.

- Rants — Get energetic, work yourself up, say what's on your mind, and tell it as is it. Rants are great for starting discourse and causing a little contention; they can likewise be very fun If you destroy them the correct soul. Simply know when you write energetically about a questionable topic that others are probably going to comment in a similar manner. Tirade posts lead to blazing in comment threads and to people making statements seemingly out of the blue that they later lament, and that can affect their notoriety. Continue with alert.

- Inspirational — On the other side of the irate tirade (and not all rants must be furious) are moving and persuasive posts. Tell an account of success or illustrate "what could be." People like to hear good news stories in their niche since it rouses them to persevere with what they are doing. Find instances of success as far as you can tell or that of others and spread the word.

- Research — In the beginning of ProBlogger, I composed many research-oriented posts where I'd do reviews or gather insights on various parts of blogging. Research posts can take a lot of time, yet they can likewise be well justified, despite all the trouble if you think of interesting ends. Present your findings with a decent graph and with helpful measurements, and you'll frequently find different bloggers in your niche will link up to you.

- Collation posts — These are an unusual mix of research and link posts. In them, you pick a topic that you figure your readers will find supportive and afterward research the thing others have said about it. When you've discovered their opinion, you unite everybody's ideas (frequently with short statements) and tie them together with your very own couple comments to draw out the common subjects that you see. These posts are frequently very interesting to readers, however, can assist you with building associations with others' blogs who you statement and link up to.

- Prediction and review posts — We see a lot of these toward the end and start of the year when people do their "year in review" posts and take a gander at the year ahead and anticipate what developments may happen in their niche in the coming months. Expectation posts will frequently cause interesting debate.

- Critique posts — Numerous bloggers have made a name for themselves by writing solid studies of others, products, or organizations. Despite the fact that sometimes these fringe on being "assault posts" and have rant-like characteristics, a good helpful scrutinize can be a successful method for making an impression upon others. People like to get thoughts, and Despite the fact that they may not always agree with them, if they are wise, productive, and respectfully composed posts, they can prompt you developing your notoriety in a niche.

- Debate — I used to cherish a good debate in high school; there was something that I very delighted in about setting up a body of evidence either possibly in support of something. Debates do well on blogs and should be possible in an organized manner between two people, between a blogger and "all comers," or even between a blogger and… themselves. (Attempt it; contend both for and against a topic in one post. You can end up with a really adjusted post.) Probably the most straightforward approach to do this is essentially to ask your readers an inquiry with at least two other options and see what they must state. Be happy to impart your very own insight to get things moving.

- Hypothetical posts — "Imagine a scenario where" or theoretical posts can be very fun. Pick something that could happen down the track in your industry and start to unload what its ramifications would be. "Imagine a scenario where Google and Yahoo. combined?" "Consider the possibility that Canon discharged an update to xyz camera?" These posts can actually position you well in search engines if the theoretical circumstance actually happens.

- Satirical posts — Well-composed parody, spoof, or diversion can be unfathomably incredible and is brilliant for producing links for your blog. Remember that sometimes these types of posts will be misjudged, and people will respond firmly.

- Memes and undertakings — An image is an idea that spreads, an "idea infection" as Seth Godin would depict it. In blogging this can be viewed as an article or topic that gets duplicated starting with one blog then onto the next, usually with a link back to the originator. Write a post that by one way or another includes your readers and gets them to imitate it in some way. Start a poll, an honor, a competition, or request that your readers present a post/link or run a review or test. These types of posts add an element of interactivity to your blog and sometimes can become a web sensation through the blogosphere.

This isn't a thorough rundown, but instead only a portion of the types of posts that you may get a kick out of the chance to toss into your blog's mix. Few out of every odd one will be suitable for all blogs or bloggers, however utilizing beyond what one format can include a little zest and shading to a blog.

Chapter Ten

Steps to Writing a Successful Series on Your Blog

One powerful method for gathering momentum on a blog is to write a series of posts that build upon each other and investigate a topic over a number of days. Writing a series will give readers motivation to return to your blog over some undefined time frame, yet it will likewise empower you as a blogger to make multiple bitesize posts on a larger topic, making the writing procedure easier yet still thoroughly covering the topic. Despite the fact that writing a series can appear to be a mind-boggling task from the outset, it needn't be. Here's the workflow that I use to make one:

1. Distinguish a topic. This is, obviously, key with regards to developing a successful series (for what it's worth with single posts). As I think about the majority of the series of posts, I've composed at ProBlogger.net over the previous year, it's interesting to see that in virtually every case the series has started in my mind as a solitary post that developed into something greater. The key is to make sure you choose a topic that is sufficiently large to warrant multiple posts (you don't have any desire to write a series only for it), yet sensible enough not to overpower you. A few topics are enormous to the point that they could nearly be a blog all by themselves.

2. Write a list. At the point when I make the decision that a topic is large enough for a series, I start with a meeting to generate new ideas and accumulate a list of the main points that I need to make. These lists generally start out as bullet-point lists of keywords and expressions reviewed either in a text record or a scratch pad. When I have a list of main points I at that point return and add a couple of enlightening sentences to

everyone to portray what I need to state. It's stunning what number of these sentences make it into inevitable posts. I find that once I'm on a roll a lot of it just streams and I can end up with a list of 10 or so ideas before long. The list is rarely the last list of points that I end up distributing (some don't make it and others are included), however it forms the reason for my series, with each point usually ending up as its very own post; remember we're focusing on granular posts.

3. Set targets. Now I set myself a few goals for the series and build up limits for it. Taking a gander at the list, I can generally tell what number of posts I'll have to finish it, which thus causes me to choose for to what extent it will run. I usually attempt to run them for a one-week term (starting on a Monday and ending on a Friday), however have been known to run them over longer and shorter time outlines.

4. Set up draft posts. With these subtleties settled, I at that point take the list I've made and whatever I've composed for each post up until this point (frequently only a couple of keywords and a

sentence or two) and reorder them into some draft posts on my blog. I give everyone a draft title (frequently changed later) and simply leave them each there as drafts for me to work on in the coming days.

5. Pick a series title. The name that you give your series is an important factor in its success and I would recommend that it be something you give genuine thought to. The title of your series is an ad to readers and will draw them into it. Readers settle on early introductions whether they will read a post, and they do likewise with a series. If you don't catch their creative mind with the primary post of your series, they are probably not going to read those that follow. The best approach to pick the title for a series is quite similar to the way toward choosing one for singular posts and is frequently a mix of something that is snappy and something with some good keywords in it (for SEO purposes).

6. Declare the series. As yet all my work is in private, however I put the weight on myself currently by reporting the series with an early on

post. This fills a number of needs, including telling your readers what's in store. (It makes some expectation.) It additionally makes me accountable for completing what I've started. There's in no way like telling your readers that you'll be writing X number of posts on a topic to keep you propelled and accountable for the assignment. Urge readers to buy in to your feed now so as to follow your post.

7. Write an introduction to the series. The declaration post will likewise incorporate an introduction to the topic. It incorporates where you'll be going over the coming days. (You might need to name the real topics you'll cover.) The other thing that this post will do is to help highlight the "need" that the series will address. I'm a firm adherent that the best series of posts that I've composed have been popular on the grounds that they meet a type of need that people have, so help readers to perceive any reason why tuning into your blog in the coming days will be important.

8. Write a post for every day. My workflow is to write posts in a series regularly. A few bloggers want to write them all ahead of time, however I like to keep them new and to not just build upon what I've composed the earlier day, yet what readers have written in the comments on those posts. I likewise find that writing a lot of posts all without a moment's delay can be excessively overpowering; breaking it down into reduced down pieces is substantially more reasonable for me.

9. Interlink your posts. I see a lot of bloggers attempting to write blog posts as a series however not getting their posts together with links. Despite the fact that your present customary readers will have the option to follow your post by signing on every day or reading it in RSS, future readers of your blog probably won't have as a lot of karma. They frequently come in by means of a search engine to a center post in the series and If you haven't linked to the rest, they will need to go searching for it. You can interlink your posts effectively enough by linking to them

all on the early on post to your series and by linking back to that introduction toward the start and end of each post (telling readers that they'll find the full series there). On the other hand, you can link to the former and next post in the series in each post, making it like a chain starting with one then onto the next.

10. Finish your series well. Despite the fact that it may sound evident to finish your series, I believe it's important to do this well. If you don't have an unequivocal end, a series can fail close to the end and a few readers will feel that they've been left hanging. Condense the series and the main points and welcome readers to include their very own points, sharing what they figure you may have missed. Learning the specialty of making a good series is something that can carry a lot of life to your blog. I attempt to do one at any rate once every month, and I find that readers generally react to them well overall. They work especially well If they are instructing focused, reasonable, and associated with a genuine need that your readers have.

Building an Interactive Blog by Encouraging Comments

The beauty of blogging is that it is conversational in nature. You as a blogger start the discussion and others react in comments on your blog or in posts without anyone else. Work with this and write such that welcomes others to take an interest, and you'll grow a progressively unique blog. Here are a couple of fast tips on getting more comments for your blog:

- Invite comments — It sounds too easy to possibly be valid, yet people are bound to comment when you ask them to. Give a call to activity to comment, and people will.

- Ask questions — Including explicit questions in posts certainly gets higher numbers of comments. This is especially the situation when the question is solicited in the title from the post.

- Be open-ended — If you state everything there is to state on a topic, you're less inclined to hear others including their thoughts since you'll have covered what they may have included.

- Interact with comments left — If you're not willing to utilize your very own comments section, for what reason would your readers? If somebody leaves a comment, interact with them. Doing so shows your readers that their comments are esteemed, it makes a culture of interactivity, and it gives the impression to different readers that your comments section is a functioning spot that you as the blogger esteem.

- Be modest — I find that readers react to posts that show your very own weaknesses, failings, and the holes in your very own insight as opposed to those posts where you seem to be knowing it all there is to know on a topic.

- Be dubious — There's not at all like controversy to get people commenting on your blog. Obviously, with controversy comes hazard and the potential for being assaulted, so use with alert.

- Reward comments — Reward good comments by highlighting them on your blog. Drawing attention to your readers who use comments well attests them, yet in addition draws attention of different readers to good utilization of your comments section.

- Establish limits — Occasionally the comments section on a blog can descend into something of a quarrel. Set up limits in advance on what is and isn't acceptable in comments. You even may get a kick out of the chance to post this as a comment approach. At last it is your blog and the standards you set are dependent upon you to choose. Having limits will assist your readers with knowing what is and isn't acceptable and can help you in your comment directing.

- Shape your blog's culture — I am progressively mindful that bloggers set the tone for their blog's "culture." It is important to take note of that readers will usually take your lead with regards to the tone they use in comments. If you write posts in an irate and personal assaulting style, hope to see this reflected in your comments section. If you model an increasingly comprehensive and friendly style, the majority of your readers will follow your lead in this too.

Don't get excessively down if people don't comment on your blog with great frequency. Indeed, even the most popular blogs tend to pull in just around a one percent commenting rate on them! Continue with the first methods, and you'll build a blog that develops in traffic, yet one that genuinely connects with people and develops a culture of network.

Blog Income and Earning Strategies

There is no single right way or incorrect approach to earn money from blogging. If you contrast the methodology Darren utilizes and the one I use, you will see a significant unmistakable distinction. Cast your net wider, and you will be unable to find two bloggers who make money identically. This is a good thing! The open door is there for any blogger to make some money, and to do it in a style that works for them. Each blog and each blogger are unique. The open doors change depending without anyone else capacities, the open doors exhibited by the niche, and even your own particular audience. Despite the fact that few out of every odd blogger will accomplish the tremendous paydays that a few bloggers accomplish, there are numerous bloggers doing pleasantly through the tactics I portray in this section.

Time to Make Money?

The principal decision you need to make is clearly whether you even need to have a go at making money. There are numerous bloggers who stay away from any kind of commercialization of blogs, and afterward there are other people who attempt to don't care for it. I will accept you would like to make money off your blog. The two questions at that point become:

- When? what's more,

- How? When to monetize is a question with no right answer. Make an inquiry or two and you will get numerous frank answers, none of which helps without a doubt.

There are two prevailing camps of opinion on this question, the two of which have their very own benefits:

- Run ads from day one — The idea here is in case you're thinking of running ads eventually, you should coordinate them from the start. The reasons you should do this incorporate the following:

  - Reader expectations — Starting a blog without any ads and afterward including them later means running the danger of disillusioning readers whose expectations are that the blog is and always will be "promotion free." Some readers feel firmly about this and changing the principles mid-stream can cause problems. Start with ads from the earliest starting point, and you set the expectations from the start and don't cause any upset later.

  - Consistent design — Running ads from the earliest starting point of your blog keeps everything predictable, which is good from a reader-solace and branding point of view, and furthermore means that you don't require the issue or cost of a redesign later on to oblige ads.

- Earnings — Darren's blogs were promotion free for quite a long time until he executed AdSense; he lamented his defer later, subsequent to seeing what he could have earned. Put ads on your blog from the start, and you'll start to see some money from the good 'ol days. Obviously, it probably won't add up to a lot, however you could be enjoyably amazed.

- Ad-improvement experience — It requires some investment to learn how to change ads. The vast majority of us learn best through personal experience instead of by simply reading about it. The great thing about starting ahead of schedule with advertising is that you can test and attempt various procedures without an excessive number of people seeing the mix-ups that you make en route. This means when the traffic starts to come in, you can have your ads advanced to exploit it.

• Establish readerships and afterward run ads — Rather than put ads in directly from the start, there is an equally legitimate contention for keeping them off until you have built an audience. This contention is basically that If you put ads on your blog too early, you might kill people your blog since it will look too business or like an over the top money grab. The idea is that you can gradually include promotions later once you've set up some trust, gathered a sizeable readership, and you have built up lots of good-quality links that serve to upgrade your search-engine perceivability.

Factors to Consider

How would you realize whether to hold off with the ads or put them in place at the present time? When choosing which way to deal with use, think about the following:

- How commercial is your niche? I used to possess a photography blog about a type of camera called a DSLR, consequently I named it DSLRBlog. People who follow the topic tend to be vigorously into hardware and in this way, ads are not simply endured, they are practically empowered, so directly from the start I would include promotions and subsidiary links in reviews. Different niches will be hostile to commercialism and subsequently a lighter touch will be required.

- Is it worth it? You may find the main advertising you can appear from the start is ineffectively paying, untargeted AdSense. If you are getting just a couple of snaps a day at some small sum per click, you may find there isn't a lot of point in including advertising until you have an audience and the content to allow you to earn from it. Much of the time you can utilize your advertising spots to show partner ads or advertising for friends to make your blog increasingly appealing to potential paid sponsors, yet it is worth considering as a major aspect of your decision.

- Will ads degrade? If your essential monetization system is to utilize circuitous strategies or sell your own product, you should focus on utilizing your blog land for those channels. Additionally, you need to think about how cheap the promotions tend to be in your niche. People are considerably more liable to disregard monstrous advertising in a set up blog than another one. You don't have any desire to harm any youngster trust you are building with off-putting ads. Once more, choosing whether to show ads is a personal decision that is driven as much by monetary weights as personal taste. Fortunately, there is no set in stone answer, and the nearness of ads is never again held in as a lot of doubt as years back.

eCommerce

You may hear eCommerce defined as "selling online." We're going to limit that definition to prohibit the advanced preparing and information products you may make and sell, just as your services. For our motivations, an eCommerce business is any business where you're selling a physical product over the internet.

Your product could be toys, clothes, food, books, books about food – anything that you need to physically dispatch. This is a popular alternative for people who are attempting to take offline businesses online, but at the same time it's significant to any individual who can connect with a network who is interested in your products on a blog.

Do's

1. Make yourself an asset for something other than the product. What does the product do in terms of taking care of a problem or making a pleasure? Become a specialist regarding that matter and make your blog a place where your potential customers can come to learn. For example, assume you sell lovely, durable wooden canes which are suitable for people who need a cane for therapeutic purposes or for help. You could offer assets on choosing a cane, just as how to think about a wooden cane and how to measure for a cane.

   You could make content on living with a disability, brief or perpetual. You could write contextual investigations about your customers and record how they utilize your canes to enjoy a full life and the amount they enjoy utilizing an alluring cane instead of a revolting metal cane from the medication store.

2. Value things carefully. Remember that all of the work you do, from blogging to shopping must be repaid by the income you make from selling. Margins in eCommerce can be low, and knowing your margins to the penny will assist you with making a profit as opposed to a loss.

Don'ts

1. Don't trim your margins to the point where making a profit is a question mark. If the main explanation somebody ought to choose you is that you're the cheapest, reconsider. It is anything but a supportable selling point except if you're Walmart or Amazon. If you separate on value, somebody can always undermine you. You should be the best of whatever you sell, not the cheapest.

2. On the surface these sites appear to be a good method to get new customers, yet it's never worth it. For starters, you make almost no money. The

discount site expects you to offer at any rate a half discount on your product or service. Groupon or any similar organization at that point takes half of what's left. Best case scenario, you make 25% of your standard cost. You may make a touch of money offering a service, however when you offer a product margins are already thin. You could well end up assuming a loss just to bring in a lot of traffic. You can't make up a loss in volume, regardless of how much volume you get. You likewise presumably won't get many repeat customers. Deal of the day buyers are usually pursuing the deal and not searching for another place to shop.

3. Don't forget that it's easier and less expensive to sell another product to a current client than to draw in another client. Make a special effort to give absurd client care. You'll see more repeat customers and referrals and spend less time and money on showcasing to bring in new customers.

Best Practices

Make sure there are contents on your website to interest your visitors than just the products index. Give quality content that interests, interests, informs or motivates your readers. Make your blog an ordinary goal, not only an index. Remember that they are not as put resources into what you sell as you may be and may esteem it in an unexpected way. Run tests on pricing, depictions and determination to determine what your audience needs to buy and what they need to pay for it.

Attempt to make bundles or groupings of your products that you can offer at various rates – include more an incentive by sparing delivery for your customers! This is regularly known as packaging. At the point when you group, make certain to ascertain your margins and make sure you're not pricing a bundle for short of what you're willing to selling it for.

Make open doors for your customers to connect with you and your content. You don't have any desire to be a supporter. You need your audience to converse with you, and you need to converse with them. Make a network as opposed to simply one more shopping site.

Is eCommerce the Right Model for You?

For eCommerce to be directly for you, you should have a physical product to sell so as to think about this model in any case. Like partner deals, eCommerce works best with a large audience. You may make some money when your audience comprises of two or three thousand people, however as your audience develops, so will your eCommerce business.

Chapter Eleven

Blog Promotion and Marketing

Going from zero to a tolerable size audience is probably the hardest piece of blogging. Although a few people appear to find their sweet spot easily and in a split second, getting an audience is something the vast majority of us need to work on. Content is critical; it is the foundation of a good blog, yet you still need more than that. A few people will tell all of you need is good content; shockingly, the truth is somewhat more mind boggling, and I wouldn't recommend attempting the "build it and they will come" formula.

As I like to state, content may be king, however without opulent clothes and a military to back him up, what is a king yet a self-important guy in a clever glossy cap?

Success in blogging means having great content backed by strong promotion — in any event until your audience is large enough that your readers' word of mouth does the promotion for you. A blog won't make you a lot of cash if no one reads it. In the wake of writing content, promotion is likely the second most important action of a blogger. This section takes you through how you can pull in readers and, equally important, how to keep them.

Building Readership

As I said in the introduction, content is critical. All things considered, that is the thing that people will go to your blog looking for. There is day by day, run-of-the-mill content; there is foundation or pillar content; and afterward there is lead content.

Building a Content

Magnet Anyone who has visited my chrisg.com blog and downloaded my free digital book knows about the term lead content. Essentially, it goes well beyond minor blog posts and works as a draw to your blog. It draws in people, since it gives an asset, a reference; something noteworthy that is worth talking about. When propelling your blog, in addition to lead "fascination" content, you need a good foundation of strong evergreen content. Darren calls this content "pillar" articles. A pillar article is usually an instructional exercise style article that intends to show your audience something helpful.

Generally, they are longer than 500 words and have lots of reasonable tips or advice. This evergreen type of article has long haul claim, remains current (it isn't news- or time-dependent), and offers genuine worth and understanding. The more pillars you have on your blog, the better. Try not to surge this part; all the other traffic systems depend on you having something valuable to visit. Looking at the situation objectively, what use is driving huge amounts of visitors to something that is inadequate or not valuable? While advancing, attempt to keep your blog new with valuable posts.

The important thing here is to show to first-time visitors that your blog is updated sensibly regularly, so they feel that If they return, they will probably find something new and worthwhile. If they think they have depleted your blog's convenience on the primary visit, they will not bookmark or buy in to it. You don't need to produce one post for every day all the time, yet it is important that you do continue refreshing while your blog is brand-new. When you get footing, you still need to keep the crisp content coming, however your dedicated audience will be additionally forgiving if you delayed down to a couple of posts for every week. The initial hardly any months are critical, so the more content you can produce right now the better.

Blog Relations

Word of mouth is critical in advancing blogs. You need your blog to be significant and spreadable. The primary thing to sift through is your blog name. Utilize an appropriate domain name if you can, in light of the fact that the easier your URL is to remember, the more probable it will be recalled. Attempt to get a .com if you can in light of the fact that that is the most widely gotten domain, and focus on small, easy-to-remember, infectious domains instead of whine about having the right keywords.

Requesting Links from Bloggers

Emailing bloggers for links can work if you do it gently and respectfully. Fail to understand the situation and, best case scenario, your email will be disregarded. Bloggers get many these types of emails; the more popular your blog is, a greater amount of them you get. Sheer amount and low quality signify such messages getting a poor reputation. Presently I make it clear that I react to not very many, and I rarely answer to them. Never at any point have a link request email as your first conversation with a blogger. Become acquainted with them first. Try not to be amazed, either, if a blogger that you think you realize well disregards your link requests. You have a greatly improved possibility of success If you follow this advice:

- Be human — Talk to bloggers as people; the more robotized the email feels, the more probable it is to be erased.

- Be honest — Don't lie and state you have cherished a site for quite a while that you just barely discovered. If you do actually like it, tell them why. Far better, tell them how you would improve it (without being annoying). I giggle each time people say they have been reading one of my brand-new blogs for a considerable length of time. Duplicity, regardless of how well intentioned, is a terrible method to start a conversation.

- Be explicit — The more dubious you are, the more probable I am to not trust you. Do your research and avoid sweeping statements.

- Be courteous — Demands don't wash. The other blogger doesn't owe you anything. All the expense is theirs, and the majority of the addition is yours. You are sending a modest request; make it read that way.

- Be interesting — You need to sell your proposition. People won't link to you since you inquire. There is a high probability your email will not be read past the initial not many lines, so make them count.

- Be meriting — Harsh yet obvious. OK write about something no one will ever find interesting or valuable since somebody beseeched you to? Shouldn't something be said about your article will the blogger and their audience find interesting, helpful, valuable, or engaging?

The key point is to be interesting. Shouldn't something be said about this proposition should the other blogger find interesting? "Since I asked" doesn't work. Picture what you are giving the other blogger to work with. You have to have an interesting story to write about and have the option to spell out how that is the situation.

Gaining Attention through "Link Baiting"

The term "link baiting" (additionally observed as single word, "link bait") is utilized by webmasters to portray an assortment of practices, all of which look to create incoming links to a website or blog from different sites. It is actually a troublesome term to be complete about in light of the fact that it covers a lot of various practices, extending from running honors or competitions, writing snarky assault posts on high-profile bloggers in the desire for them gnawing back and linking to you, through to furnishing different bloggers or site proprietors with valuable tools. As a general rule the term "link baiting" is another term for something old.

On the Web links are currency; along these lines' webmasters did all they could to get links from the most punctual days of the Web.

Successful Link-Bait Ideas

It is difficult to concoct a complete list of what these practices are, on the grounds that they are restricted distinctly by your creative mind! All in all, every strategy utilizes a "snare" or some type of curiosity. Utilize the following list of ideas for inspiration:

- Tools — Create a valuable, fun, newsworthy, or cool tool.

- Quizzes — Quizzes, overviews, and personality tests, for example, "Which Star Wars character are you?" have long been popular with web clients.

- Competitions — Organize a challenge or drawing with a valuable prize.

- Scoops — Be first with the news or to take a stab at something new.

- Awards — Create an honor for your niche.

- Lists — List the 10 best blogs in your niche, or the top products, etc. Seek glossy magazines for inspiration; they are full of lists

- Statistics — Do a review and discharge the results. One of my customers used to do a worldwide study moderately modestly that got them monstrous attention.

- Freebies — Give away something of significant worth.

- Interviews — Interview a big name or somebody popular in your niche.

- Resources — Create a definitive asset or reference for a topic

Two benefits of running competitions on your blog are:

- New readers — Competitions are potentially good for drawing new readers to your blog If you have an approach to get the message out.

- Reader tenacity — Knowing there is a competition result to come keeps people from leaving; else they will not check whether they won.

The dangers with competitions are:

- Distraction from common content — Your standard visitors don't come to see competition content, so they may get disappointed.

- Few champs, numerous failures — You can't supply a prize for each member, such a significant number of people will be disappointed.

My very own involvement in competitions is that if you design your competition well, you can get the benefits without the drawbacks harming excessively. Here are a few hints:

- Build an audience — Although competitions can produce traffic, you have to have a critical mass of readers before propelling so as to build cooperation.

- Identify goals — Before you design your competition you have to work out why you're having it. What is your point? By what means will you measure the competition's success? When you have your goals, you would then be able to make better decisions about the competition format, prizes, promotion, etc.

- Offer prizes — A number of musings strike a chord when choosing prizes for a competition. Prizes ought to be:

- Relevant — Match the prizes that you offer to your blog.

- Worthwhile — The better your prizes are, the more buzz you will potentially make.

- Affordable — Don't spend so a lot of that you won't recover the worth.

- Use supports — One approach to impart the heap to a competition is to have a supporter for it. If you have a nice size readership, you may have the option to find a support essentially by asking.

- Use member links — To help spread the expense of prizes, choose prizes that you can promote utilizing associate projects.

- Make necessities attainable for members — Don't make members pay some dues.

- Make necessities reachable for you — Competitions can be difficult work, and people anticipate reasonable play. Don't make things more troublesome than would normally be appropriate.

- Make simply entering valuable — An additional motivating force could be a free link to all members, or simply being something, they get fun out of in addition to a possibility at winning.

- Set a reasonable competition length — You don't need it to delay for such a long time that your readers become tired of it, however then again,

164

you need it to be long enough for readers to enter, for the word to spread about it, and for patrons to get their money's worth.

- Promote your competition — Unless you promote it, nobody will realize your competition is happening. Start your promotional endeavors with your very own readers by means of your blog, and furthermore let your blogging friends know ahead of time. The best competitions have a component for those taking an interest to spread the word here and there; for instance, if they allude a friend, they get additional passages in a draw.

Chapter Twelve

Search Engine Optimization for Blogs

The Web is full of great content that will never be seen outside of the creator's screen. This is on the grounds that the writer has neglected to comprehend that only a couple of simple changes in the blogging procedure can expand search-engine perceivability. Numerous people attempt to paint search engine optimization as a dreadful spammer strategy: "gaming" search-engine results for their very own shrewd ends.

This is simply not always the situation. Like any amazing asset, it very well may be utilized for good or shrewdness. Search engines are tied in with giving clients the most relevant results. Good SEO helps that; awful fills the engine with spam. People regularly ask me how to get positioned number one for a specific search result. Lamentably, the only people with conclusive answers work for the search engines themselves, and they are not talking.

The best advice for people needing to enhance their blogs for search engines is to start with quality content on a particular topic and afterward change it utilizing the ebb and flow best practice. Despite the fact that SEO can appear to be entangled and baffling and can become something of an obsession for blog proprietors, you should realize that, as a general rule, blogs are not exactly well set up for SEO directly off the bat. Search engine optimization techniques fall into two general classes: offsite and on-site techniques.

Off-Site SEO

Off-site techniques are, as the name proposes, factors from outside the site that impact the blog's ranking in search engines. Huge numbers of these factors are outside the blogger's control; notwithstanding, they are helpful to think about. The most clear and likely generally ground-breaking off-site factor is inbound links. It is generally agreed that the links that point to a website are one of the most compelling ways of climbing search-engine results. To put it most simply, every link to your site is seen by the search engines just like a demonstration of positive support in your site.

The best inbound links:

- Are from highly positioned sites.

- Are relevant to your topic.

- Use relevant and searched-for keywords. Obviously, you don't always have control over who links to you, yet when you do have an influence over how you are linked, these are the types of links that you ought to focus on.

Step by Step Instructions to Generate Quality Inbound Link

So how would you get such looked for after links? Presently you know why we spent so a lot of book space on examining leader content and link lure! Here are some more contemplations on the most proficient method to pull in quality links:

- Offer valuable content — The most ideal approach to get links to your blog is to write quality content that people will need to read. You can request links with others, pursue diverse link-building programs, or even buy text links on different sites, however the cheapest and presumably most secure methodology is to build inbound links in a characteristic, organic way, as others link to your quality content.

- Notify relevant bloggers of your content — Though I don't advocate spamming different bloggers and asking for links, I do recommend that If you write a quality post on a topic that you realize will interest another blogger, it may be worth giving them a short and respectful email telling them of your post (see the past section on blogger relations).

- Use indexes — An old method to create inbound links was to present your links to catalogs. I am aware of webmasters who still depend on the results of such a procedure, yet I think the benefits are usually small, best case scenario.

- Inter-link your blogs — It is worth taking note of that you ought to be careful with this methodology; if all your sites are hosted on one server, many imagine that search engines will work out what you're doing, and the impact will be decreased.

- Buy links — Many professional webmasters have a budget to buy links from other highly positioned and relevant sites. This is a costly and high-hazard system.

- Swap links — A more seasoned system is to trade links in a "you link to me and I will link to you" way. Be careful with this; the procedure has a poor reputation because of spammers mass-mailing link-asking messages and other awful practices.

On-Site SEO Techniques

On-site techniques are things that you do on your own blog that help build a higher ranking. Likewise, with all SEO techniques, there are numerous tactics and a lot of speculation around every one of them. Recognize a couple of keywords for your article that you might want to be found in the search engines. What will visitors type into Google if they need information on the topic you're writing about? The response to this question will give you a clue with respect to what words you'll need to see repeated all through your article a number of times. These keywords will should be sprinkled all through your article.

You can highlight keywords in the following ways with differing levels of influence on search results:

- In the URL

- Titles

- Links, in and out

- Bold text

- Heading labels (H1, H2, etc.)

- Image alt labels

- Throughout the text of your post, especially at an opportune time, in the initial not many sentences obviously, if you go over the top with keywords it will demolish your article. Don't forfeit your readers' understanding of your site only for SEO.

Truly, keywords can be important in improving search-engine rankings, yet increasingly important is to guarantee your content and design are easy to understand and accommodating to readers. A site that is loaded down with keywords will show up spammy, so don't fall for the temptation. Utilize inner linking to expand the perceivability of different articles in your blog and utilize good keywords in the stay text. Additionally, make sure every page links back to your main page and some other important pages on your site. In case you're writing on a topic you've recently expounded on, consider linking to what you've composed previously or utilize a "relevant posts" include at the base of your article.

As a rule, you need each article to be focused on one topic. The more firmly focused the topic of a page, the better where search engines are concerned. Sometimes you may find yourself writing long posts that end up covering a number of various topics. They may relate freely, however If search-engine ranking is the thing you're pursuing it could be smarter to break up your post into smaller, increasingly focused pieces. Maintain a strategic distance from copy content however much as possible.

Google in its guidelines warns publishers to have the same content across multiple pages. This applies to multiple pages you have and to pages outside your site. In fact, spam tactics are usually to reproduce content on numerous pages or steal content from other sites. There is some discussion about what duplicate content includes and what it includes, but the best advice is to pay close attention to the number of places your content appears.

Increase Page Views on Your Blog

Just as getting new visitors, it is important to keep visitors interested. Keeping your readers drew in and coming back is similarly as important as finding new ones. Insights have revealed that the average blog reader views around one and a half pages every time they visit a blog. The more pages a run of the mill visitor reads, the better the activity you are doing. What would we be able to do to get readers to see more pages? How about we investigate a couple of conceivable outcomes:

- Highlight related posts — One of the more common practices of bloggers to encourage readers to read multiple pages on their blogs is to highlight related posts toward the end of your article.

- Interlink inside posts — A similar however maybe progressively effective procedure is to highlight relevant posts inside the content of your posts. In case you're writing a post that mentions something similar to what you've written previously, simply link to your past post from inside your article.

For instance, I've written about this system already in a post on expanding the longevity of key posts.

- Highlight key posts and classifications in your sidebar — Highlighting your category pages is another helpful procedure to encourage your readers to find more posts on a similar topic. To expressly name what your category is can likewise be helpful. That is, instead of simply having the category name toward the end of the post, have a go at something like "read more posts like this in our XYZ category."

- Create compilation pages — Many first-time readers utilize these pages to discover content to read. Every post a visitor reads expands the odds that they will become faithful readers.

- Write a series — You should be careful with writing series of posts over timeframes; however, they are a great method to keep readers coming back, and once they are finished to have them surf through multiple pages on your blog. Don't make series only for expanding page views, obviously — this can really baffle readers — however use them on longer posts or when you truly need to cover a larger topic over time.

- Use selections — There is always debate over this topic. Would it be advisable for you to show the full article on your homepage and feed or scraps? If you only have halfway content unmistakable, the reader needs to navigate to see the full thing. Despite the fact that this is positively an advantage of fractional feeds, doing so will make a few readers unsubscribe to your blog totally. This is a cost/advantage situation that individual bloggers need to gauge.

- Be interactive — An effective method to get readers coming back to your blog many times over a day is to have a blog that people need to interact with.

Build Community and Get More Comments

So, 1% of your blog's clients are actively captivating with your blog, and the rest are, best case scenario occasional contributors. The examination isn't simply on blogging, so the genuine numbers could be pretty much than these and would no uncertainty fluctuate from site to site at any rate, however the guideline remains constant. Most by far of readers leave a blog without leaving a comment or contributing to it in any capacity. Somewhat this is only the manner in which it is, and we most likely need to simply become accustomed to it;

however, with regards to comments there are a few ways to encourage greater interactivity on your blog:

- Invite comments — Regular readers of my blog will see I frequently welcome people to comment, with an expression, for example, "What do you think? If you don't mind share your considerations in the comments." When I specifically welcome comments, people leave them in higher numbers than when I don't. Remember that new readers that are new to blogging don't always think about comments or how to utilize them, and sometimes people nearly should be given permission.

- Ask questions — Including explicit questions in posts unquestionably gets higher numbers of comments. I find that when I remember questions for my headings, it is an especially effective method for getting a response from readers since you set a question in their mind from the principal snapshots of your post.

- Be fragmented — If you state everything there is to state on a topic, you're more averse to hear others including their thoughts, since you'll have covered what they may have included. Despite the fact that you don't have any desire to intentionally leave such a large number of things implied, there is a craftsmanship to writing open-ended posts that leave space for your readers to be specialists moreover.

- Be interactive — If you're not willing to utilize your very own comments section, for what reason would your readers? If someone leaves a comment, at that point answer. This gets harder as your blog develops, however it's especially important in the beginning of your blog since it shows your readers that their comments are esteemed, it makes a culture of interactivity, and it gives the impression to different readers that your comments section is an active place that you as the blogger esteem.

As the movement in your comments section develops, you may find you should be marginally less active in it since readers will start to take over on responding to questions and making network; however, don't totally overlook your comment threads.

- Be modest — I find that readers respond very well to posts that show your very own weaknesses, failings, and the holes in your own insight instead of those posts where you seem to be knowing it all there is to know on a topic. People are pulled into humility and are bound to respond to it than to a post written in a tone of someone who may cruelly respond to their comments.

- Be thoughtful — Related to humility is elegance. There are times where you as the blogger will misunderstand something in your posts. It may be spelling or syntax; it could be the core of your contention or some other part of your blogging. At the point when someone leaves a comment that shows your bombing it's very easy to respond cruelly in a defensive way. We've all observed the blazing that can result. Despite the fact that it is difficult, an elegant way to deal with comments, where you concede where you are incorrect, can bring out the prowlers and make them feel somewhat more secure in leaving comments.

- Reward comments — There are numerous ways of recognizing and "fulfilling" good comments that range from "reader appreciation" posts through to highlighting especially good comments in different posts that you write. Drawing attention to your readers who use comments well certifies them and furthermore draws the attention of different readers to make good utilization of your comments section.

- Make it easy to comment — I leave a lot of comments on a lot of blogs every week, except there is one situation where I rarely leave a comment even if the post deserves it — blogs that expect me to sign in before making a comment. Possibly I'm apathetic (actually — there's no perhaps about it!), or perhaps there's something inside me that stresses over giving out my personal subtleties, yet when I see a comments section that requires registration I quite often (95 percent or a greater amount of the time) leave the blog without leaving the comment that I need to make.

Despite the fact that I totally comprehend the temptation to require registration for comments (fighting spam by and large) something inside me opposes partaking in such comments sections. Registration is an obstacle you put in front of your readers that some will be happy to jump however that others will shrug off (the equivalent is regularly said about different comments-section necessities that go beyond the fundamentals). Keep your comments section as simple and as easy to use as would be prudent.

Chapter Thirteen

Social Media and Your Blog

You can't have missed the developing buzz around "social media" over ongoing years. It appears the television and paper media are fixated on Twitter this and Facebook that. Maybe this fixation is on the grounds that the traditional media dread the new media as competition?

At its generally general, social media envelops every kind of social or network site, however each service or tool can be extensively classified as "Social Bookmarking," "Media Sharing," and "Social Networking." This part shows you how you can utilize these different social media tools furthering your potential benefit.

Determining Which Social Media Sites to Use

Choosing which social media site to utilize depends largely on your goals and where your audience hangs out. Your most wanted result determines which tools to utilize and how you interact with them. Social media services can deliver breathtaking benefits to you and your blog, and they are especially good for standing out, and for engagement. With attention you will potentially develop your links and subscribers, and with greater engagement you will extend networking connections and hold more dependability.

The confusion emerges when attempting to make distinctions, since all of these sites are blending features, with all social media sites allowing you to include friends, and most sites urging you to share or rate content. In terms of promotion, the main draws are social bookmarking sites, for example, Digg.com, StumbleUpon, and del.icio.us, and the high traffic media sharing sites, specifically YouTube. For networking you would hope to Twitter, Facebook, and for business networking or work seeking, LinkedIn.

Social Bookmarking

You know when you find a helpful site that you expect to require in future, you bookmark the site in your browser, so you have an easy method to allude to it. Social Bookmarking started out as an approach to share your bookmarks, so as opposed to sitting on your computer you have them wherever you go, and your friends can get to them as well. The most celebrated of these sites is presumably Delicious.com however Delicious has melted away in popularity and acclaim, for the new breed lead by Digg.com. Every one of these sites can possibly send you a large number of visitors, and they all work by individuals submitting content and allowing others to pass judgment on it or decision in favor of it somehow or another. Getting popular on these services has transformed into an obsession for some bloggers, which can be hazardous when it occupies you from looking after your customary readers.

Social Networking

On the opposite side are the Social Networking sites, which are tied in with making connections among people and cultivating communication. In general, the features you expect to see on a Social Networking site or service are simply the ability to make a profile about yourself, include people who you know or discover to a list of friends, and to send messages to your contacts. A few services started out as celebrated "address books," yet once the individuals started interacting, the intrigue immediately went to having discussions and sharing links and content.

Media Sharing Services

This type of social media service blends a considerable lot of the features of the other two. Media sharing services started out as an approach to store and share your very own content, for example, transferring your pictures to online photo collections with the goal that your family overseas can see your wedding pictures. Much the same as social networking sites you can befriend different clients, and furthermore much like social bookmarking sites there is regularly an approach to rate or comment on content that others share.

Every type of computerized media has a popular service supporting it, from video through to PowerPoint presentations, if you have content there will be a place to share it.

Executing Social Media Promotion

Social networking sites can drive traffic, and a portion of the media sharing sites have staggering traffic potential, yet for promotion, the greatest traffic spikes originate from the social bookmarking services, so we take a gander at those first. To get traffic from a social bookmarking site your article must be submitted and get a lot of votes. This works distinctively for each service.

Traffic from StumbleUpon comes by means of an uncommon toolbar that you can download from its site. On the others you have to sign in, find the fitting article, and afterward hit the bookmark or vote button. Since there are such huge numbers of services it is ideal to focus on only a couple. I mainly focus on StumbleUpon on the grounds that with only a couple of votes you can get a decent progression of traffic. I have friends who focus on Digg on the grounds that, Despite the fact that it is far harder to get obvious, when your content gets to the front page you get a tremendous traffic spike.

Writing for Social Bookmarking Success

Social users usually browse. They don't want to spend a lot of time figuring out if something deserves attention:

- Write attractive titles.

- Passages are short and blunt.

- Use bullets, images and subtitles to facilitate skimming.

- Draw interesting quotes and key points.

- Turn it into something that people want to talk about, share, or give back.

Engaging Your Followers with Social Media

Social media isn't just about creating traffic and getting attention. It can likewise be a key method to keep your audience interested and steadfast, build your brand, and produce all the more networking chances. Numerous people presently hope to Twitter, and Facebook as not simply places where to monitor the most recent exercises of friends, yet in addition as a replacement for the traditional blog news channel. I am a case of this.

At my pinnacle I bought in to over 800 feeds in Google Reader, however now I monitor feeds only occasionally and rely on Twitter to deliver scoops inside in the niches I monitor. Most likely a considerable lot of your readers will utilize these social tools in a similar manner, so having a nearness and grabbing your brand names as a Twitter account and Facebook vanity URL is worthwhile. In addition to sharing your most recent headline, you have to interact with people and treat them as individuals instead of only a wellspring of snaps. This means having conversations and sharing cool content regardless of who made it, not simply your own.

Utilizing Twitter

Twitter was originally a service that allowed you to give "Announcements" through responding to the question "What's going on with you." But while that was what it was intended for, it is presently utilized in the following ways:

- Chatting

- Getting help and replies

- Sharing links

- Getting news refreshes

- Making friends and networking

- Marketing

- Sending and accepting reminders

- Getting mechanized alarms

- Worshiping famous people

Essentially it has become a combination of news source, tattle center point, and catchall text informing system. My own relationship with Twitter has transformed over time. From the outset I didn't get it, I thought it was a narcissistic exercise in futility. At that point I gave it another possibility, and fell in love with it, however more importantly thought that it was very helpful.

Twitter is accessible from its website, Twitter.com, by means of work area programming services that work with the system, and through a portable web version for keen cell phones. You can connect your email address, include your cell/cell phone number, and get text messages through the system. The most popular Twitter customer is at present TweetDeck.com which is accessible for Windows and Mac work area, and furthermore the iPhone.

The Three Great Non-Social Uses for Twitter

Twitter isn't only for talking with friends. There are additionally genuine benefits for probloggers and businesses:

- Inside scoop — Follow the correct business insiders and you get the news before some other channel. I have accessed information and beta accounts along these lines, and it tends to be very helpful.

- Traffic — Drop a link with a good introduction and you can see click-throughs and comments as a result. Track what number of people clicked a specific link utilizing a service, for example, Bit.ly, which just as shrinking the web address down to a progressively sensible size, likewise counts snaps, and who shared the link. You get even more traffic and followers by being "Retweeted" where others share the message you posted, so encourage others to share your links by retweeting theirs!

- Networking — I have expressed commonly how important networking is for bloggers. Twitter is a developing venue for this with less obstructions and guardians. Make sure you link to your Twitter account from your blog and from your email mark to encourage people to follow you.

Facebook

While Facebook started out as a very young environment, the statistic has widened now to incorporate essentially anyone. Truth be told, with a cited 350 million clients, with 35 million people signing in every day, Facebook now has a day by day client base that smaller people the population of numerous whole countries. Much like a blog, Facebook allows you to refresh your account with notes, video, photos and links, in addition to like Twitter you can post short "notices" to tell your friends what you are doing.

In addition to ordinary client profiles, anyone with a business or a tremendous fan base can likewise make Facebook Fan Pages. With a typical client account, you are restricted to 5,000 friends, however with Facebook Fan Pages there is no restriction to the number of contacts you can gather to a page. Commencement your Facebook following by linking from your blog and from other social media accounts, for example, your tweets. The key to Facebook success is to share cool stuff and to encourage friends to share your stuff with their friends to get a viral impact moving.

Chapter Fourteen

Planning for Sustainable Growth

S ince you've done all the research, planning, and actualizing, it's time to consider one last thing: what's your arrangement for developing your business after this first product or service? This is another of those territories that gets investigated when people talk about monetization. We've set up that you can never treat your audience or community like an ATM, however neither would you be able to forfeit growth to warm fluffy emotions. This section will show you how to deal with your growth over time.

What is the Meaning of Growth to You?

In terms of your business, what is the meaning of growth? It's useful to pose yourself some questions about growth and money. For instance:

- How a lot of cash do you need?

- When will you say no?

- What will make you state no?

- Is there a limit to what amount of money you need to make?

- How big do you need your business to be?

- What number people do you need on your team?

- What will your team members do?

- How much would you like to work on your business and in your business?

- When will enough be sufficient for the life you need?

- When will you feel that your business is too big and taking an excessive amount of time and vitality?

You may take a gander at these questions and think you have no idea what the answers are, however, you most likely do. You know yourself, and you comprehend what you really need. You know how you need your life to be and what you need from your business. Be honest with yourself about the answers to these questions, even If you think someone else would answer in an unexpected way.

For instance, maybe you have determined that you could, by selling products, arrive at seven figures in five years. However, you realize that if your business develops to seven figures, you'll have to hire several team members and you'll have to work basically full-time. You likewise realize that you need to work 25 hours per week and have close to one or two people working with you. In this case, you choose that seven figures aren't some place you need to go.

You're glad making in the mid-six figures with a menial helper and low maintenance software engineer on your team to help deliver advanced preparing. These questions may appear to be overwhelming, however you already know the answers in case you're willing to remember them.

Scaling the Mountain

Scalability alludes to your ability to develop something, in this case your blog business. For instance, an advanced instructional class is very scalable, in light of the fact that once it's made, you can sell it to numerous people. Once you have the wrinkles worked out of the preparation and have a client care system that can handle more customers, you can build your number of customers over time.

Your time, on the other hand, isn't scalable. You can physically only work such a significant number of hours a week, and this limits the number of instructing customers or service customers you can take on at some random time. We should take a gander at a couple of more things that are and aren't scalable. Physical products are scalable. You can continue to sell an ever-increasing number of products, if you have the client service limit and you or your provider can handle more requests.

Partner products are scalable, if the product proprietor is fit for taking care of more deals in terms of client assistance and in terms of supply of physical products.

Computerized products are scalable, again depending on client service capacities. Membership sites are scalable if you have the data transfer capacity and plate space accessible to handle the heap, just as the client support needs of your community.

As we said previously, training isn't scalable. You can scale instructing to a degree by offering bunch training, however there is a limit to the amount you can extend bunch instructing. You can't include an unending number of people to each gathering. Consulting and other personal services are not scalable. You can charge more for your time, however you don't have an unlimited measure of time you can work with customers.

Planning Your Growth

You're not going to reach your long-term objective immediately - it will require some investment, perhaps as long as several years. You have to set shorter term, quantifiable goals, and stop and evaluate once you reach them. For short-term goals, it's a good idea to look three to six months beyond where you are today.

At that point set longer-term goals for every year. If you evaluate your advancement every three to six months and every year, you ought to have a good handle on how your business is growing and what you need to do to slow or build growth.

Things to Consider

There are a few things you have to consider when you plan your growth.

To start with, would you be able to go it alone? You in all likelihood can from the outset, yet when will you need assistance? Plan ahead of time for this. You don't have any desire to scramble to hire someone once you need them and have to bring them up to speed rapidly on the grounds that you have an emergency.

You always need to hire someone before you need them and have them prepared and ready to assume control over their obligations without a deadline or emergency approaching.

Do you need more power? We're not talking about personal position, however website hosting power. Is your hosting ground-breaking enough to withstand a huge number of website visitors a day? Do you have to switch now?

Do you realize where you will go and the amount it will cost when you are ready to switch? What will growth resemble?

How would you expect your growth to happen? Will you increase gradually, selling more products gradually?

Will you spend additional time, exertion and money on advertising and grow quick? What will you have to do to handle your growth?

Will you have to work with providers to make sure they can handle request? Will you have to get more client service help? Would you be able to bear to grow? Will you have to acquire money to handle inventory as you grow? Do you have the assets to hire help and meat up your web hosting capacities? Do you have the time to grow your organization?

Will you have to leave your place of employment if deals reach a specific point, so you can run your business full-time? These are all questions you ought to consider in determining how and the amount you need to grow.

Chapter Fifteen

Secrets of Successful Blogs

What do you understand by "success"? For every blogger it will be something other than what's expected. It could be acclaim, income, deals, size of audience, etc. Even however Darren and I consider ourselves professional bloggers, we both arrived at it through our very own courses and tactics. We earn money in various ways and have various goals. At the point when you take a gander at different bloggers in this part, you can perceive how diverse professional blogging really is. Before embarking on a blogging venture, it is worth discovering what success would intend to you.

Analysis of Top Blogs

At the point when we took a gander at the top blogs and bloggers around us, we discovered there were sure elements in common between them, paying little heed to niche, monetization technique, and motivation. Specifically, age, posting frequency and social media all appear to focus intensely in their success.

Blog Age

Darren did some research some time back and discovered that the average age of the best blogs was 33.8 months. The primary lesson to remove is that blogging is a long-term thing, however it is conceivable to have success a lot quicker with karma and a lot of difficult work.

Posting Frequency

In many examinations of top blogs, a prominent trend is that the best bloggers post more than the rest. Usually they post many short posts a day. There appears to be an unequivocal correlation among success and posting frequency. It makes sense; the more posts you distribute, the more possibility for links and for readers to see you.

Search engines likewise prefer to see lots of crisp content, feeding as they do on text.

This can cause alarm for bloggers who battle to keep pace. What you have to remember is that the majority of the top blogs are written by multiple writers. Team blogs can without much of a stretch keep up a high post rate, and frequently need to if they are in quickly changing news niches, for example, TechCrunch.com.

Of late, however, there has been a backlash against too high a posting frequency, with bloggers and readers both communicating an inclination for less, better-written and well-considered articles. In numerous surveys on the question of why readers unsubscribe, "posting over and over again" usually positions high.

Revenue

Most by far of successful blogs show advertising, with not exactly a quarter utilizing Google AdSense. It is worth taking note of that when blogs get to this kind of scale, they have the traffic and audience to request excellent deals, even from Google. A significant number of the top blogs currently hire advertisement salespeople, utilize the services of specialist promotion organizations, for example, Federated Media, or are a piece of blog networks. At a specific size, a blog turns into a business by any definition, so they tend to work that way, with CEOs, editors, and writers.

Blog Language

You may expect English to rule blogging overall, however in terms of volume, Japanese takes the top spot with 37 percent, and English is second with 36 percent. With regards to the Top 100, however, 80 percent are written in English.

Learning from Niche Blogs

We have already recommended in this book that you at least start out blogging in a niche. The bloggers in this section have made their blogs so highly focused and so identified with their topic that they are the leaders and standard-bearers for their chosen topic.

- Strobist.com — A photography blog that, rather than focus on the whole topic of photography, went super-niche and wrote about using small, inexpensive flashes. Now David Hobby has been able to take a leave of absence from his job as a photojournalist and is earning money through running workshops and developing his own range of training products.

- CopyBlogger.com — Lots of bloggers write about blogging; Brian Clark decided to start a blog about the art and techniques of writing. Initially writing on his own and then bringing on guest writers (Chris included), CopyBlogger is now the most-popular blog on the subject and has been used as a platform to launch Brian's Teaching Sells online course.

- Lifehacker.com — Productivity is a massive subject online, and Lifehacker is probably the best known. Rather than just write about productivity in general, Lifehacker approaches the subject with a techie slant, which the audience really enjoys.

Lessons from Niche Bloggers

1. Distinguish an underserved niche — It is very hard to get a photography blog saw in today's blogosphere. David Hobby picked a miniaturized scale niche, a niche of a niche, and served it comprehensively with his Strobist blog. Make it easy on yourself and choose a niche where you can make a distinction.

2. Characterize your blog's mission and well-spoken it in a benefits-drove way — If a reader sees your blog's mission and thinks "so what?" you have fizzled. Be certain your blog's mission helps the reader.

3. Possess your mission and remain focused — It would be so easy for any of these blogs to consider their to-be audience as permission to cover anything they like. Once in some time they can pull off it, sort of like a pop star choosing to discharge a swing collection. To an extreme, however, and the valuable and unique quality that pulled in readers could leave.

Lessons from ProBlogger

1. Be first — There was a time when it was easy to have first-mover advantage. Clearly, that was when barely anyone had the foreknowledge to start something besides a personal diary blog. There are a large number of blogs now regarding each matter; by what method may you be first? Be extraordinary. Find an opening and fill it. Demonstrate the upside of your unique take.

2. Staying power — It is alluring to hear of six-figure incomes and become despairing at your very possess small Google check. Darren didn't arrive medium-term either. A portion of my biggest slip-ups in blogging have been stopping, cutting, and advancing. Don't make my missteps; learn from Darren. Stick with it!

3. Hotshot your best stuff — Put your popular stuff front and focus where people can see it. Exactly when you visit this blog, you are not lost for things to read. After people read your post, do your readers know where they can go straightaway?

4. Community counts — Great content is important, however when it is gotten together with a lively community, that is the point at which your blog will genuinely take off.

5. Test and research — Blogging is a moving objective. Working out what works and which tactics don't take research, experimentation, testing, and exchange. Consistently, Darren investigated various avenues with respect to new developments from MyBlogLog.com to Chitika.com. Make sure you remain mindful of the times.

6. Security — Don't uncover an overabundance of personal information. Choose what you are going to keep private, and make it remain in that capacity.

7. Remain positive — I don't think I have ever observed Darren go off on a tirade. This builds up a tremendous measure of goodwill. You will never hear a dreadful word said about him. Blogging success is as much about networking as it is good writing.

What Causes Ideas to Spread?

If you consider the last time you told someone something you heard, it will probably have been the following:

- Different/New — People don't discuss things that are common and standard. People consider things that are new or different. English Cut (Figure 10-1) was the principal blog about men's suits anybody had heard of; start a blog like that today, and no one would pay heed.

- Newsworthy — News is probably the biggest type of information to spread, however that doesn't always mean it is new or different. Sometimes it is the idea of the story that causes it spread. Sometimes conventional things can become news If they happen to someone important.

- Easy to comprehend — If you need to ponder something before you get it, it will as a rule appear an excess of exertion, regardless of whether you think it is important somehow or another. Streamline your message, and it will spread all the more successfully

- Easy to remember — How will people spread your ideas if they can't remember them? It's much the same as jokes; a few of us have an ability for remembering and letting them know, yet despite the fact that I love to listen to a comedian's recount to complex stories, I can review and retell just the most fundamental.

- Easy to communicate — There is a good reason why politicians utilize sound chomps; they are easy to remember and convey. Make it easy to get the point over. Provide "send to friend" and bookmarking features.

- Beneficial — Will your story help someone? Will it make them chuckle? What will the sender and beneficiary addition? The more advantageous, the more it will spread; personal circumstance quite often becomes possibly the most important factor.

Useful-Blog Properties

We will all have different answers, but if we put together the properties of these favorite blogs, I would expect to be able to group them into one or more of the following categories:

- Fun: Blogs are increasingly used for entertainment. People come to them to laugh, gossip and have fun talking.

- Educational: Some blog readers are primarily interested in learning something new about a particular topic.

- Informative: Many successful blogs are thirsty based that some should be informed about a problem, product or topic.

- Reflective: Some blog readers want a place where they can open their minds and engage in good dialogue, discussion, or even combat issues.

- Latest News: Many blog readers just want to be updated in one area.

- Community: Some very successful blogs exploit the need to connect and belong with people. Very often the issue is secondary to these connections.

Conclusion

Author's Final Thoughts

Thank you for reading this book till the end and now that you have been exposed to the nitty-gritty of how to set up your blog and monetize your blog, I hope that you turn those words into action and see to making your first couple of money via blogging.

Nothing good comes easy. Be strategic about your blog and make sure to use the techniques provided in this book.